# RECONNECTING DISCONNECTED GENERATIONS

Abraham A. Great

# CONTENTS

Dedication.................................................................7

Acknowledgements.....................................................8

Introduction..............................................................9

**CHAPTER 1**

UNDERSTANDING GENERATIONS...................13

**CHAPTER 2**

DISCONNECTED GENERATIONS.....................23

**CHAPTER 3**

THE BABY BOOMER GENERATION..................33

**CHAPTER 4**

ADVANCE TO BE CONNECTED.........................43

**CHAPTER 5**

RECONNECTING THE DISCONNECTED.........49

**CHAPTER 6**

THE ART OF WORSHIP.......................................55

**CHAPTER 7**

THE POWER OF THE WORD...............................69

**CHAPTER 8**

FALSE SENSE OF INTIMACY..............................75

**CHAPTER 9**

SPIRITUAL OBLIGATIONS........................................................79

**CHAPTER 10**

STAY FOCUS AND AVOID DISTRACTION..........................97

**CHAPTER 11**

GET CONNECTED TO GOD.................................................119

# DEDICATION

---

I am dedicating this book to my late father – **Rev. Joshua Olukunle Akintayo.** Your courage to withstand the cold hand of death when it struck your son at age 13: 'Undignifed' in the eyes of those around that day, you set your feet dancing and prayed around the corpse. Daddy, today your son is growing from glory to glory doing what you saw before you went 'home' to be with the Lord. I will always love you. Thank you for giving me the chance to live to fulfl God's purpose for my life.

# ACKNOWLEDGEMENTS

Someone once said 'One is too small a number to achieve greatness'. I totally agree! For this reason, I would like to thank the team of people God has placed around me; those who have made it their goal to help accomplish my mission. To my wife Queen - you remain the only person who is able to accommodate all my proclivities. You have always had the strength to do what I cannot do while I focus on what I can do. To my Four Boys - your dynamism inspires me to write songs, books, articles and sermons. You guys are a good team in the' Great household'. I love you! To all the staff and volunteers of GR8TERWORKS, HE LIVES BIBLE CHURCH, STR8T RECORD- you guys respond to my ideas and ideals without tiring- without your input, we wouldn't have had this manuscript.

To my father and role model, Bishop David Oyedepo: I am extremely grateful for the values you have taught, lived and continue to exude. You indeed are a man of value.

To my personal pastor, brother and great inspiration, Pastor David Oyedepo Jnr. - your wisdom is valuable for the accomplishment of my Divine Task- thanks. You and your siblings are a unique example of how values could be passed from generation to generation.

# INTRODUCTION

This book has taken critical study of different generation and how they have managed their relationship with God, it focuses on how different people of different generations has responded to the advancement happening in their society, it also explains how Satan has distracted Christians from the things of God by injecting worldly affairs in different generations

Some of the key generation considered in this book are the why-errs, millennial, subconscious mind. I believe as you read you will get insight to affect this generation positively in Jesus name.

At the end of reading this book I strongly believe that you will discover the generation you belong to and by so doing you will encounter God afresh and reconnect totally to him without succumbing to the tricks of the Satan that distracts saints from the things of God with the things of this world.

Are you feeling "down" today? Are you discouraged because of your experience from yesterday? In an unguarded moment, did you stumble and fall by yielding to sin? Do you need a reconnection with your maker? I think we all reach points in life where we need a clean slate.

Its crystal clear that this generation is suffering from a setback caused by the total disconnection from God, we have totally forgotten the pain Jesus Christ went through on the cross, even though we are advancing technologically and becoming smart and scientifically upgrading but we still have drawn away from the life of God which was the main aim of creation.

There is something worse than falling down; it is staying down. The wicked fall and shall not rise, but with Christ it is not so. Though we do sometimes fall, we will not be content until we are restored. We should not sin, but too often we do.

The apostle John wrote, "If we say that we have no sin, we deceive ourselves" (1 John 1:8). But here's the good news: Jesus chirst He goes on to say, "These things I write to you, so that you may not sin. And if anyone sins, we have an Advocate with the Father, Jesus Christ the righteous.

Admit your failures. Don't worry over them, but confess them. Jesus died for us because He knew that we would continue to struggle with sin, so He made provision for our daily cleansing.

Start fresh each day by taking time to confess your sins, to admit your weakness, and to ask God for His strength to do what He wants you to do. As you depend on God's Grace and strength, you will soon know what victory really is!

Thankfully, God's Grace helps us in our life to reset. resets in our life. He loves us unconditionally and His desire for us is to turn to him; no matter how hard we try, how much we deny, or how far we've gone, we can't get resets without God. I've found that God will never allow my heart to stay far away from him, so he is always working to guide us back to Him. Sometimes, He does this by allowing us to get to

The point where we really see that what God wants is better than what we want. This is the beginning of a turning point – when we begin to desire what God wants more than what we want.

I think God also loves giving us resets because they not only help us, they also inspire people around us to turn to Him. When other people see what God can do in our lives, they get hope that

He can do the same for them!

Maybe you need a reconnection in marriage, a new beginning in parenting, or a do-over in friendships. God will always reconnect all our disconnection in the areas we need them. In the book of Isaiah, the people of Israel needed a reconnection in their relationship with God. They had reached a turning point, and God gave them three steps to take to return to him:

"Prepare the highway for my people to return! Smooth out the road; pull out the boulders; raise a flag for all the nations to see." Isaiah 62:10

Living a life of true faith comes with its own set of challenges and questions. We all have seasons of doubt, or at the very least we've been in a place where a little bit of clarity could go a long way in fully understanding what it means to be a follower of Jesus. There's that sense of feeling stuck as you wrestle through questions like:

- Who is God and what is grace?
- Is unconditional love a real thing, and what happens when life gets messy?
- Why is a relationship with Jesus so important, and why does He care about me?

# CHAPTER 1

# UNDERSTANDING GENERATIONS

*There is a generation that curseth their father, and doth not bless their mother. There is a generation that is pure in their own eyes and yet is not washed from their filthiness. There is a generation, O how lofty are their eyes! and their eyelids are lifted up. There is a generation, whose teeth are as swords, and their jaw teeth as knives, to devour the poor from off the earth, and the needy from among men. Proverbs 30:11 -14*

Blessings flow from fathers to children; and when a son returns them with a curse, it is the worst of crimes. Secondly, those who are pure in their own eyes. Being proud and ignorant, they guard the outward walk but cherish the foulest evils of the heart. Hence there is little hope of doing them good. The third and fourth are the haughty and the cruel, who scorn and oppress the poor. They are far from humanity, and therefore far from God, who will pay them back the measure they deserve.

We live in an era whereby things are happening beyond our human control. Some of us seem to be spectators of the event occurring meanwhile others seem to be actors or pioneers of the event occurring. Whatever be the case we have one or two roles to play in the event happening around us. We no longer live in an isolated Island, we are mutually connected, being it directly or indirectly. Though we seem perplexed and confused unable to live a regular life like a clock on the wall. We would rather stand still and gaze at life event happening in sequences. Even our human spirit is reassuring us that something is wrong somewhere, somehow things are not right. Something seems to be wrong! what is the problem? Who is responsible for all the happenings around, are there people involved or is it as a result of our collective actions.?

Sometimes we seem dumbfounded living in a world where someone can't even differentiate what is right or wrong. We accept whatever comes our way like the standard of life, confused because we see impossibility rather than a possibility. Confused because we see the world in a vast point of view and without thinking that our actions can have a multiplier effect on all the events occurring in our society and world today. We misguided Confused because even those we rely on seems to be falling us and there is none to trust. We are indeed confused and who shall come to our rescued?

It is on this note that I have chosen to observe the devastation of our modern world culture ethics and values, this made me consider putting this book into your hands and by believing that my role and your role will make a tremendous impact upon our dying world. The world is crying and waiting for nothing else but for people with renewed mind and spirit like me and you, to take action for the restructuring our generation and preserve the future generation. The world and the creation at large are in an anxious state waiting for the sons of God to manifest. They are waiting for them to manifest that creative ability in them by taking actions that will put things in the right way.

King Solomon in the book of Proverbs said there is a generation who curseth their father and refuse to bless their mother, there is a generation who sees themselves as pure yet had never washed away their filthiness, there is a generation that sees them high in dignity and character, there is a generation that is so wicked like a knife to slay away what the poor and the needy have. A generation whose leaders are never satisfied with their ill-gotten wealth yet the masses and poor remain poorer. A generation in which mercy is far from the heart of the leaders and the innocent are victims of the crime committed to them. What a generation? This is what John the Baptist observed in his dispensation and he couldn't stand it rather than to cry and say "Ye serpents, ye generation of vipers, how can ye escape the damnation of hell?" He went further by saying such generation won't escape the damnation of hell as well. He was hurt and angered because of the devastating situation that took place around his periphery. It is with this same spirit and passion that I am angered in my spirit to talk with you reading this book; Godly anger of cause. I wish to talk with you reading this book that there is a generation whose life is at stake, a generation whose lives has been dubiously taken aback by the media world.

There is a generation whose children's morality is in constant decay. There is a generation whose leaders don't border about the masses but about the stomach and egoistic drive. There is a generation whose politician deems it necessary to deprive the wealth of the poor. There is the generation who don't have respect for humanity and shedding blood to them is a game of fun. There is a generation whose Christian values, standard and foundations have been neglected. There is a generation who wholeheartedly stands to correct the bible to favor their turpitude aims, there is a generation who don't care of voting evil into power and thus enacting homosexuality, bestiality, and pedophilia as the pride of life. There is a generation that stands to correct the human race by recreating themselves that is men are turning into ladies and ladies and are becoming men. These generations need you, they need your aids, they need your action, they need your support. They're groaning and crying for you to rescue them. God has heard them and is saying whom shall I send?

The main purpose of this book is to illuminate some shady part of your life so as to bring about positive transformation in our society and country at large. There are many of such generation and some have classified it into a different category; However, in this book, I have termed them in the simplest way that would enable you have deep understanding and then help you benefit from. Some of the generations highlighted are The GI generation, the Baby Boomer Generation etc.

However, there are six types of generation and each differs from each other in terms of their attributes, likes, and dislikes. People have been structured and group into general generations, characterized by similar qualities and attitudes. According to sociologist Karl Mannheim explained generations as "a group of individuals of similar ages whose members have experienced a noteworthy historical event within a set period of time". He also noted that "social change can occur gradually, without necessarily bringing in major historical events, but those events are more likely to occur in times of accelerated social and cultural change". Each generation has collective experiences and similar ideas. The importance of classified humans into generational groups is to help us understand their targeted characteristic and problems. This classification has benefited the media, sociologist and many others because each generation feels and act differently regarding a wide range of issues.

Sociologist analyses the following generations; In the 20th

Century, there were four (4) generations, which are **the greatest generation, the baby boomers, the generation X, and generation Y.** These generations were subdivided into sub-generations. The greatest generation was subdivided into the GI generation and the Silent generation. The GI generation is the termed "coined by coined" by American journalist Tom Brokaw to describe the generation of people who grew up during the deprivation of the Great Depression, and then experienced the World War II (1901- 1924), as well as those who made productivity contribution within the war's home front. This generation is considered as those who save the world and build nations. They had a strong belief in morality. This made them not to have any reason to embrace the uncultured and ungodly doings of this present days, they are role models to themselves. They believed marriage for life and no divorce, there wasn't anything like gay marriage and all related vices, they had strong loyalty to their jobs and there was no retirement. You worked till you die. They were natural, they enjoy life without airplane radio or the media. They attained greatness with these attitudes which made them qualified to be referred to as the greatest generation.

"Every time you do a good deed you shine the light a little farther into the dark. And the thing is, when you're gone that light is going to keep shining on, pushing the shadows back. Charles de Lint

The silent generation is made up of the generation who experienced the WW II in their childhood and experienced the civil right movement (1924 -1945). It also includes most of those who fought during the Korean War... This was an era when Women stay at home as a housewife and if they were to do any job that will be jobs like teaching, nursing, and secretary. They were very disciplined, self-sacrificious and cautious. The children that were raised during this era were focused and hardworking. They speak

17

less but rather believe in doing more to make a difference in the society.

The next generation we have is the **Baby Boomers generation.** They are the people born between (1946 – 1964) during the demographic Post-World War II baby boom. They are labeled as 'baby boomers' because there was a high birth rate during the post-war event. There was a steady increase in the number of children born especially in America; there was an approximate figure of 3 million babies born each year within this time frame. This developed to the increase in youthful age group and up-rising adult life which as a result lead to an economic boom which everyone enjoyed but it also encompasses a euphoria lead to the subsequent rise of events like cold war, civil right movements, terrorism, shooting of leaders like John FK and the pope 1983, the imprisonment of Nelson Mandela in 1964, the Vietnam war, etc.

During this period there was a great political and social change in government all around the globe. Those who don't conform to the norms and values of the society were easily labeled as the nonconformists. Some of their actions were experimenting with drugs, sexuality, renewed increase in women's preferences, increase in rock and roll music. This generation was self-centered and self-righteous. These ushered in the idea of free love and nonviolent societal issues. They had strong desire to change the common values for all and they were optimistic and believe in teamwork. They also had respect to hierarchy and authority. They envision the upcoming technological advancement and experience the first TV. The media was born! It was in this generation that the first divorce was experienced and they also began accepting homosexuality. They started the idea of retirement and started to enjoy their life as they wanted. They were the first to explore and started space exploration.

The 4th generation we will study in this book is the

**generation X.** Generation X was the termed coined by the Magnum photographer Robert Capa in the early 1950s. Magnum is a photographic corporation and community of thought that shared human quality, a curiosity about what is going on in the world, a respect for what is going on and a desire to transcribe it visually. This was the generation born between 1965 - 1980s. This generation is subdivided into two that is the baby Busters generation and the MTV generation.

The **baby buster generation** is the generation of people born 1965 and 1980. This is the generation of people who experienced the increased of mass media, the cold war, and the Vietnam war. They were born before 1973 and spent most of their teen in the 1980s. Most of this generation are children of The Baby Boomers and The Silent Generation. This generation, unlike the Boomer generation, is those that emerge from the from a significant birth rate decrease in the population. They are very community oriented most of them came from single-parent home. They are often scared to marry even though they had a hunger for relation. According to Fortune magazine, they are very entrepreneurial and prioritized personal achievement. They have a spiritual hunger and often in deep need of hope, also involved in organized religion. One of their technical achievements is the computer.

Under the generation x, we also have the MTV Generation. This generation was highly influenced by the MTV in the late 20 and early 21 centuries. These are the generation of people born between the mid-70s and 80s. The term has been widely used to describe the generation of young people in a western world influenced by fashion trends. The teen of this generation who grew up in the 90s has been tagged as the doom generation due to the popularity of the 1993 game Doom.

There is also the boomerang generation under generation x. This word is coined by the press to describe, sometimes disparagingly, the children of the baby boom. This is the generation of Young adults in western culture. It is named as such because of the frequency with which they choose to cohabitate with their parents after a brief period of living on their own – thus boomeranging back to their place of origin. This generation places their parent under serious financial trauma by living at home at the age of 20 to thirty. According to a study by Pew, statistic shows that 36% of ages 18 to 34, had returned to the family fold. What a disconnection! There is a great need to sensitize and built such youth with a value system and ability to reshape and develop. Generation X has experience horror childhood due to divorce, latchkeys, political corruption, wars, violent movies, etc.

**The Y Generation:** The Y generation; they are also known as the Millennial, Echo's Boomers, and Generation Why? Most researchers use commentators use birth years ranging from the early 1980s to the early 2000s meanwhile others described them as the people born between 1977 and 1998 (approximately 70 million people). However, defining the birth dates causes a global debate. Many countries have their own dates how our aim here is to have a comprehensive understanding of how things work so we can by the grace of God restructures what need to be structured and to benefit from what we need to benefit from in each generation. Generation Y has been raised in within the period that they are constant access and increase in technology. This generation has seen the rise of mobile phones, laptops, computers, etc. Companies and firms have change adjusted their hiring strategy in this generation faced with constants technological advancement. They are seeking on how to attract and retain the best candidate while taking into consideration technological advance.

Unlike generation X, members of Generation Y are more technologically savvy because they are growing up within the Information Age and are prone to use media in everyday life.

They can easily be controlled or led astray by the media. It has pros and cons. They are expected to create a cultural shift and are flexible with schedule. This generation is willing to learn and explore new things. They have respect for authority and there is a falling crime rate. With unlimited access to information, they envision the world as a 24/7 place and prefer working in a more relaxed environment. This generation has benefitted from greater parental attention than the past in generations and more fathers are involved. Somehow there is a risk that the media might be controlling them than their parents. If we as parents or individual take a deep look into this generation, we will be able to build a generation of genius.

**The generation Z:** this is the generation born after 2001. They are the savvy consumers of all the latest technology and they are tired of brands. There is a high probability that they will live a highly sophisticated world composed of media, computer and internet savvy than the previous generation. They are a generation more involved in social media and they believe strongly in it.

Since my kids belong to this group, it is my responsibility as a father makes them understand that they are a chosen generation and they must live up to the standard that our heavenly father demands of them. Our final mission is to make heaven.

# CHAPTER 2

# DISCONNECTED GENERATIONS

This generation is the most advanced, most blessed of a generation that has been. But it is also the most disconnected to its origin, fundamentals, and values (so talented but also so disjointed).

Moral values are at highest level of decadence, stupidity is now making celebrities and celebrities are the new breeds' stupidity. The generation before; people became known for wisdom, knowledge, prowess as their values, while this generation people become grandiose or ostentatious just by doing anything.

Every generation seems to find what's best to communicate, the better the communication the more connected the worst people are.

The questions are:
- How connected is this generation to the past generations in form of values?
- How disconnected is this generation from the values that brought us this far?
- How disconnected is this generation from its creator?
- How connected is the church with her owner?

- How connected or disconnected are you from your Father.
- What are your proofs of connections?
- What are the reasons or factors for disconnection?

By the grace of God, we will spend the next chapters analyzing these questions, also discussing why staying connected to the God will the help of the church in this generation stay closer to God.

"Everything that is in the heavens, on earth, and under the earth is penetrated with connectedness, penetrated with relatedness." - Hildegard of Bingen

Whenever I stand on the church platform to minister the word of God there is this consciousness of generation in my mind. So, when I think with generation in mind. I think years and generations ahead. We have to think big.

*"Ye did run well; who did hinder you that ye should not obey the truth?" (Galatian 5:7 KJV)*

Preaching is a very humorous thing. Never believe a man who started prophesying by giving peoples phone number or your number out in front of about twenty-five thousand congregations. Ask yourself the question "why God would want my phone number to be given to twenty-five thousand people?" If I have been running my church on prophecy, we would have had to have the Thames Valley Police officers helping us to control the traffic in Bletchley. People like to prophesy unto, they to be told the future because they like to be cajoled or their future told to them. The lingering question is why would God need to show himself with a mere phone number in front of thousands of people, our God is more than that and he would never be involved in show off.

## PROPHESY TO EDIFY

"Prophecy is not to edify a man but to edify God." Prophecy is to correct, to instruct them. The generation we live in now enjoys hypnotism, people like to be mesmerized; we liked to be told what we don't know we have become all of a sudden very lethargic to knowledge. We like somebody to come and show us the future when we are already in the future.

The end purpose of all true prophecy is to build up, to admonish, and to encourage the people of God. Anything, that is not directed to this end is not true prophecy.

This basic purpose of true prophecy is stated in 1 Corinthians 14:3:

*"He that prophesieth speaketh unto men edification, and exhortation, and comfort." (KJV)*

*But everyone who prophesies speaks to men for their strengthening, encouragement, and comfort. (NIV)*

If for instance, you feel like you should share an edifying Scripture with someone and aren't sure you can rest assured sharing the Word of God is never wrong. So be free to share the Word in an edifying way. It may be for the present moment or for a future day. Trust Him and be obedient. Edification is always good.

Galatians 5:7 said "you ran well. Who hindered you from obeying the truth? In other words, it began to say that you started well but who has hindered you from obeying the truth. This generation is most advanced, most blessed than any generation that has been but it is, however, the most disconnected and ignorant than any other generation before us. This generation is also the most misinformed and far from the fundamentals. Many children and many homes have left basic morals, basic etiquettes of living.

Nowadays we see young folks doing all sort of acts far from morals, so many youths in this generation are involved in drug dealings, sagging and all forms of immoralities but still termed it as fashion anyone against such act is seen as not fashionable, People are living in promiscuity and they refer to it as enjoyment, and if you do not participate in their type of enjoyment they called it out of order. Our generation has moved from phase to phase so rapidly that we don't even know where we are today.

Disconnected! Though talented, it's unfortunate the generation is completely disjointed, moral values at the highest level of decadence, and stupidity has become our new value. Stupidity is now making celebrities famous, who in turn are the new breed of stupidity, it has grown to the level that once any stupid act is done you automatically become a celebrity with so many followers all over the internet and all over the social media just because you have just done something stupid and you instantly a famous personality.

Our society has grown to a level whereby you two people are having a catfight removing each other's clothes and you have millions of people hitting on likes that to make it a hit, exposure over the internet turns them into instant celebrities become famous. This made me reach the conclusion that becoming famous in this generation is too cheap and you only have to be stupid to achieve fame or celebrity status When did we get to this? When stupidity has become our next value and when the state of ostentatious being that somebody is exhibiting foolishness. Disconnected indeed!

The previous generation was known for wisdom. They were known for prowess. They were known for values and their contribution to society and humanity, but this generation you are known for nothing. Today you see names that are making millions and when you ask them what have they done or know, they simply tell you they do nothing. They simply advertise their body in the name of beauty. We now see abnormality as a new link, the devil is pumping his vices in to the world and tis generation are embracing it with all joy. Thereby reducing the number of saint to be raptured with Christ. People sometimes seem to be cowards.

They cowardly follow others, not because of anything special but simply because the masses or the media is following them. Such people have actually abused a position of privilege and other misdemeanors. They have given themselves to the god of this world who control them in many facets including whatever they see. May God save this generation! This generation has become grandiose, they become ostentatious and if we as a church do nothing, we'll hand it completely to the devil.

Malcolm X once said, I quote: "The media's the most powerful entity on earth. They have the power to make the innocent guilty and to make the guilty innocent, and that's power. Because they control the minds of the masses."

Let take an example of how people communicated about say 60 years ago and how it is done today. About 60 years ago, the generation before or the people in their 60s right now they connect by having a conversation. People invited others to have a conversation. They will drive to your house, as a matter of fact when a man was created and placed in the Garden of Eden, God will visit Adam to have a conversation or fellowship with him.

Today is the social media. For sake of better understanding, I am not against Facebook, as a matter of fact, God started Facebook. God wrote on the wall King Belshazzar's Wall (The writing on the plaster wall of the king's palace.) "Suddenly, they saw the fingers of a human hand writing on the plaster wall of the king's palace, near the lampstand. The king himself saw the hand as it wrote, 6 and his face turned pale with fright. His knees knocked together in fear and his legs gave way beneath him." (Daniel 5:5-6)

So, when people wrote on your wall, you usually know the person who wrote on it, the first person to write on anybody's wall was God. God was and still a specialist in writing on the wall.

Before apple introduces tablets, Gods already did that with

Moses. He wrote the 10 commandments upon tablets. No, the brand, Apple, Samsung, Sony, etc., all began with God. He is the beginning of everything and the creator of everything that ever existed. He created everything for himself and for his glory. All things have been created through Him and for Him. He is before all things, and in Him, all things hold together (Col 1:16 -17).

Now we have twitter in which we are now following people, Jesus was the first to tweet– asking people to follow – "follow me, follow me". Do you know how many people that have been following Jesus since he said those words? Jesus has the strongest and largest followership of anybody we know. Most of these things we are enjoying these days are derivatives from the bible. All these trends people are following; we need to follow them carefully and understand their origin and where they are all leading to. When you don't know the use of a thing abuse is inevitable. God created everything for himself and for his glory. Satan never created anything. The main thing here is Satan has simply perverted what has been created. He has made people abuse the use of it.

"When purpose is not known, abuse is inevitable" — Myles Munroe,

## THE POWER OF DESIRE

Through the power of Desire, a man can change the course of his existence in this world, especially a desire that pleases God. The Bible gives examples of persons such as Joseph, Daniel, Paul and Ruth who encounter with God turned their lives around. Their desire to do the will of God was crucial to their destinies.

Our destines are a function of our desires. What you don't desire, you don't deserve. Ruth was changed because of her desire to obey the God of Israel.

First century disciples in the upper room desired power and

the] y received it on the day of Pentecost. Acts 2: 1-7

Elisha asked (desired) for a double portion of Elijah's anointing and received it. Elisha saw Elijah going up to heaven and took the mantle that fell from him. 2 Kings 2:12-15

Joshua stayed at the tabernacle and did not depart because he desired an impartation from God. Exodus 33:11

David desired the anointing, power and glory of God over his life and God was with him through all his battles.

## HOW DESIRE IS NURTURED IN THE HEART OF A PERSON

By being fed up with living in fear and anxiety.

A man desires the power of God when he is fed up with negative history and experiences in life.

Desire is born where a man is fed up with ordinary or normal existence.

Desire is born by establishing a longing for fasting and prayers.

## WHAT ARE THE BENEFITS OF HAVING GODLY DESIRES?

The ability to secure the attention of God. When a man is passionate for God, it is impossible for God to look away. The word says Blessed are they which hunger and thirst after righteousness sake, for they shall be filled. Matthew 5:6

You have the opportunity to express intentions and expectations before God.

You have the opportunity to discover the requirement for power.

Godly desires connect you to the power of God. Supporting this point, the woman with the issue of blood comes to mind. "only if I can touch (desire) the helm of Jesus' garment, I will be made whole". Matthew 9: 20,21. The woman's desperate situation build up in her a strong desire and faith to receive healing from Jesus.

Desire gives you the grace to face the future. Jacob had the desire to turn his life around. " I will not let you go until you bless me" said Jacob in Genesis 32:24-28

Desires, generally is a God-given gift. It is given for us to appreciate the beauty of creation of creation. To admire and adore the handiwork of God. Whatever you don't desire it automatically means you don't deserve it. Satan knows, this principle so well that he always uses it to influence humanity negatively. It is a good thing to desire anything created by God. It is a good thing to desire, food, dress, children, woman and etc. There is nothing ungodly with desire. It is imputed in the human nature by God. What the devil does is using this desire to influence humanity and this generation. If someone doesn't have a desire for sex, you'll never see such people committing adultery or fornication. Now, you can see that it is the base of his desire that desire decided to influence such a person. You'll never have a desire to have an affair with some cattle for example. Until such a desire is to develop that's when you will people falling in such track, like bestiality, etc. Now, for a generation to be reconnected, it desires most be redirected!

## CONTROLLING YOUR DESIRE

How can one build its desire? You keep your desire ablaze and alive depending on the things you feed yourself on. The more you yield to the things around, the media and so on, the more you find yourself loving it and doing the same thing. People who are lovers of fashion and celebrities, today didn't just wake up one morning start loving them. They were influenced by the media and from there, they started following the negativity of the mainstream media.

Secondly feed on the Word of God, for it is the undiluted Word that has the power to change the way you feel and react towards things. Feeding on the Word of God gives the Holy Spirit the ultimate audacity to control your entire life and desire. A generation cannot be regenerated without the Holy Spirit. He is there to lead us and the next generation to the utmost life of the kingdom. The best person to repair a spoil car is the manufacturer because he's in possession of the spare parts.

# CHAPTER 3

# THE BABY BOOMER GENERATION

The next generation we have is that of boomers – when having children, the common saying then was "call me for us to get together" and the use of phone and telecommunication became rampant. People use the telephone so much that some became an expert because of the time devoted to their various devices

We also had a generation that wrote letters, people just love writing and this pre- causal to email. I used to live in another country on the west coast of Africa and I used to write my wife before we got married. These emails were usually sent through booksellers who currier them to Nigeria and sometimes these letters stayed in their pockets for up to 4 weeks and sometimes they overlapped. However, when she got the letters she valued them and when the booksellers come back maybe 3 months later, I valued the letter I received back too. So, we value conversation and we value one another. But these days you can be living in the same house with your friend or with your wife and not be connected because of lack of conversation this implies even though we have the best technology but we can still be disconnected.

During those days, people got married to each other for a mere exchange of flowers from one place to another, from one city to another or one country to another and the aroma of the flower will smell for the next 65 years of marriage. It's generally known that this new era you take each other to the restaurant; Nando's, McDonald's you go to the best restaurant and the girl can still say to you that I don't really know, I am not sure or I have not decided after the investments the man has made. This shows the level of how integrity has fade out of our society.

Flower was just sufficient during the time of the baby boomers, how can someone have invested so much which still result into negative response, my friend is either you decide or you vomit my investment – advanced but yet disconnected, we are living in the same house but yet we don't know each other anymore, we are in the same bed but our hearts are in different places because the transformation and advancements happening in our world can tear our heart apart. So many are married but still thinks about another lady or man elsewhere,

The value of marriage, the value of worship has eroded, degenerated and filtered down the drain in this generation. This generation has seen more people come to Jesus than any other generation. Millions and billions of people have met Jesus, yet promiscuity has never been this advanced but there is lethargy in church. This is the time we become sensitive! The question now remains are connected or disconnected?

We have the Esther, This is a thirty-five-year-old who sent me an email – this is my generation when email started I was one of the first few people who got in on the email, then I was in Senegal, I took it to Ivory Coast - I was a big man and I created a lot of email for my friends – In fact, I was employed to manage business for people coming from America, - I was creating email for people and the revenue from that was enough to take care of my siblings. I was collecting up to 10000 Naira for creating gbenga@yahoo.com for people in Nigeria before an email arrived there. The market was good, sometimes people are not satisfied with the name that has been created for them, they may want gbengusga@yahoo.com for example so they have to add additional money to be changed. I was creating an email for people and they were happy to go. My father said it was a big thing and value it greatly, we value the time spent together chatting after the long queue up at cyber cafes to use their new means of communication. My wife and I were in a relationship at that point in time and one of our friends ran a cyber café and she would go and wait there to receive an email from me. We do not mind how long we have to wait for, we valued the opportunity to chat. This was because people value connection and communication. But nowadays your husband may even send you an email and you don't even know. Your husband can send you an email that you won't even border to open not to talk about reading. Sometimes emails are piling up until your husband returned from his trip and started asking – I have been away in Nicaragua and I have been trying to reach you - "did you not see the emails I sent you" and the wife will answer – "oh didn't know you sent me some emails." Advanced but disconnected.

## THE WHY-ERRS GENERATION

Then we move to the "why-errs" - the "why-generation" – The thirty-year-old, it is text, text, text all the way. It is texting all the way but with the text, they are still disconnected. You look at yourself and at your bill, each time I observe some teenagers and take a looked at their bills or logs, some would have sent over 1000 text this month alone and some sent over 10,000 text in a month and sometimes cannot even remember the name of the person they're texting – most of the time they have to ask for the name of the person they are text because they have been on it for a long time and they have forgotten who they are texting, sometimes they will inform the other person that his or her name was just stored as number rather than the person. For example, on my Facebook page I have over 5000 friends and if you asked me, probably I know only sixty of them. Connection but at the same time disconnected, advanced but at the same time disconnected.

## THE MILLENNIAL GENERATION

The millennial generation is the one we are presently where we have advance means of communication coupled with very flexible social media to match with it, the generation whereby we have social platforms like Facebook, Twitter. I will encourage you to follow me in to the scripture.

*"You were running well. Who hindered you from obeying the truth? This persuasion is not from him who calls you." (Galatians 5:7-8 EST)*

What is that thing that has cut you away from the original thing? What is the thing that has disconnected you from the original source? Advancement is good but are you still connected to the source of the advancement? The increase is good but does this connect you back to the creator to the one behind all things.

The Millennia has been so disconnected that the people's self-esteem is so calculated by the number of people that followed or unfollowed them. So, you wrote something on the wall and nobody or a low number of people followed you, you feel down that nobody likes you. The Bible informs us that self-worth is given to us from God. He provides us with strength and all that we need to live a godly life. Our confidence comes from God

*I can do all this through him who gives me strength. Philippians 4:13*

For the Spirit God gave us does not make us timid, but gives us power, love, and self-discipline. 2 Timothy 1:7

Your definition of self-worth should not be determined or defined by the number of people who liked you or not and even people who followed you or not. So many have gotten it all wrong be ignoring valuable people in their life just because "I posted and you didn't comment" "I sent a message you didn't like it". We are advancing but we are getting disconnected! We are losing the core human values of life. Shall we allow this demeanor to continue or is there something that can be done? Perhaps we should just believe in the myth that things would change by itself or let's wait for an angel to descend and bring a change in this generation. What a dilemma! What is the problem?

"Never be bullied into silence. Never allow yourself to be made a victim. Accept no one's definition of your life, but define yourself." —Harvey Fierstein

Every generation seems to find what is best to communicate but one thing that pains my heart is this every generation has stopped asking how do we connect to the maker of all things. We did not start from our self, everybody you are connecting with either through a computer or Facebook did not start with him or herself. You were not created when Facebook was born in 2000. Therefore, Facebook cannot be the source of your joy, twitter cannot be the source of your joy, no matter what you write and for some of us that have been opportune. I have come across people who are devilishly addicted to Instagram, this is very rampant among the ladies, they spend hours looking at the different style of dress and pictures, still they never get satisfied. They ended up saying am just looking or feeding my eyes with the latest style invoke, they've forgotten Looking is not just looking at the mouth says; It is an act of conceptualization whereby you conceptualize what you're gazing on. You are in other words, meditating on it by picturizing it into your subconscious mind which later turns to control you and thus control your destiny. Do you know that your subconscious mind controls almost everything about your life? Let me explained a little bit further, so we can understand how the social media and some of the things we watch has helped transform and pervert this generation negatively.

## THE SUBCONSCIOUS MIND

Information received from the physical world is being stored in the subconscious mind. The subconscious mind processes this information without even taking note of it. It is done indirectly and this information is later retrieved by the conscious mind. The conscious mind is the alertness or awareness of being around you. It being aware. Most people are unconscious, they take actions unconscious without them knowing, it is only later they tend to regret "oh what did I do for myself. I wasn't really on my sense". Such individual is being lost or lost in the subconscious mind. The Bible instructed us to train our mind and to be transformed. When you are conscious, you will be able to direct the affairs of life with peace and at ease. Nothing won't border you because you'll enjoy life at it full. Be careful of what you feed your mind with. This generation has all sort of things that are there to disconnect you from your source.

Remember what Romans 12:2 says.

Do not be conformed to this world, but be transformed by the renewal of your mind, that by testing you may discern what is the will of God, what is good and acceptable and perfect.

## INSATIABLE WANTS

Human wants are insatiable. You can never completely satisfy your need. When you look at someone having what you don't have you find yourself wanting that. You see billionaires, for example, you think in your mind that when you get there you will never need anything because you have all the money in the world. Well, that is just a fallacy! Human ego always wants more and more and more. The human race has unlimited wants and nothing else can satisfy this need except God. For He is the complete satisfaction that man needs, without him your life or your marriage life will never be complete. They will always be a need, a need for something you cannot satisfy. For a continuous flow of electricity, the current must be connected to its source. If you disconnect from your source you won't have light. For your life to experience light, you must be connected to the source of all lives. In Philippians 4:6, Paul says, "Do not be anxious about anything, but in everything by prayer and supplication with thanksgiving let your requests be made known to God." And then in Philippians 4:19 (just 13 verses later), he gives the liberating promise of future grace: "My God will supply every need of yours according to his riches in glory in Christ Jesus. "If we live by faith in this promise of future grace, it will be very hard for anxiety to survive. God's "riches in glory" are inexhaustible. He really means for us not to worry about our future. We should follow this pattern that Paul lays out for us. We should battle the unbelief of anxiety with the promises of future grace.

There is a particular kind of car that I like to drive is Range Rover, recently somebody gave me a taste of it and once I have driven it what else? There are still some other cars I like to and once I was in America, I drove one of them again and that is it - what else? By the time you finished driving it you realized that vanity upon vanity all is vanity.

There is no amount of car you can buy that can drive you to heaven, there is no amount of private jets you can buy that will fly you into righteousness or righteous wing or into the gate of heaven. There nothing that you can acquire that can give you peace, so the path of all things remains with the source and if you are not connected to the source you will not be resourceful. Source determines the type, and your type determines your size, I give you an example, the child of a goat is a kid goat, even though it is a kid until one year old, but it is still a goat. The offspring of a dog is a dog even though it is called a puppy and it is supposed to bark. A child of a cat is a cat even though it's called a kitten. Therefore, a child of God is a god! "God said let us create man in our own image after our own likeness and let them have dominion", so if you are a child of God do you look like him and are we still connected to him, are we aspiring to be like God or things that are created by God.

Our definition of a connection is that we are connected to the time rather than been connected to the creator of time. It seems to me that the more advanced we get in communication, the more distorted we become. The better the communication method, the worst people reconnected. There's something I stumbled upon some time ago called "Facebook suicide" that is somebody committing suicide on Facebook. You get frustrated on Facebook and you commit suicide. The question now is –how connected is this generation of the past generation in terms of values, you need to ask that question to yourself always. Ask God how connected this generation is in terms of value.

Some of us grew up with values that are a privilege to pass on to our children there are so many values that even us parents are no longer living with those values. There are certain values I have inculcated in my family. Whenever any is not in a place I find it uncomfortable. In my house, it is a burden or like a depression, if my family did not have devotion before leaving the house in the morning. I feel depressed and sincerely unhappy. Do you know why? This is because of it a value that my father instilled in to all his children. We were woken up every morning, and in fact, he did it with a bell – we call the bell in my vernacular "ago igbala" (bell of salvation). The ringing of this bell was so loud that it can wake people in the adjacent five street up. So many embraced the idea of waking up early and even to pray they requested if the ringing of the bell could extend to their area, (because of the community service the bell provide, that is serving as an alarm for early morning workers) my father built a bell tower in front of the house. This bell served a dual purpose for all in the area and the church in our compound. When he rang the bell, children going to school woke up, workers going to work woke up by 4.30 am a living product of the early devotion today and I will consider it a great shame if this is not pass on to my children.

# CHAPTER 4

# ADVANCE TO BE CONNECTED

So many of us, our parents gave us money in addition they also explained to us why we have been given the money and sometimes our money is tied up to Godly activities, like paying for your tithe, offerings, sometimes for the man of God and for prayers as well. Many have lost this value, we have completely forgotten all these practices, we are no longer practicing them not to talk about passing them on to our children because our prayer life is non-existence or so flat that we do not pray unless we are told to do so or our values have become valueless. We have been handed over the value to pray and to know right from wrong.

In our generation when a child does something wrong, the whole street or community would correct or discipline the child for such wrong attitude or act. The street was so unified in its values in that sense when you put a phony dress for an example, everyone frowns on you and you will be scolded, corrected and directed from one end of the street to the other, until the information reaches the parent's house. Sometimes, the child's parent(s) would appreciate and finished the act of discipline and correction being applied to the child. Sometimes it seems like the more advanced a generation is, the more eroded is the mind of the people. People began to find solace in stupidity and excuses to watered down or do away with values and make them not invalid and stupid things become the norm.

Another question is how disconnected is this generation from the values that brought us this far? The United Kingdom did not become what they are today by chance. The original word "Brit" or to be a British means covenant which means when you are British you are a covenant person. The red on the flag of Britain represents the blood and a sign of the covenant, that is a people that are in covenant with God also in covenant with one another. This is serious business, through that covenant, they conquered the whole world by fighting for it.

Some many today do not want to fight for anything and they want victory, people are not willing to go through anything. Do you know how many bloods were shed before Britain attained the position it has today in the world? America is celebrated all over the world today but only few understand what has transpired in the past; so many don't know what it took to gain American independence. Some of us we go through a little bit of trial and we have lost the will to fight and the value of fighting for what we want, we all want a microwave destiny. We come into the church today and if what we want we get it in three months we stay for what we want next, if not we move to the next church and the next church. Someone will come into the church and will say "I know you have the word but I need a miracle I have been asking the Lord for the miracle – I need miracle".

As you are reading this right now, believe that miracle is taking place, the transformation is taking place, healing is taking place because there is power in the spoken and written word of God. God sent His Word and is Word heals and transform the generation of the Israelites.

We need to seek God the creator and maker of this Universe. A lot of people in this generation are running after the created things rather than to the Creator of the things. Such people, when they get their miracle they immediately started looking for another miracle next by and check out of that church. They are kind of Christian proselytes that move from church to church looking for miracles. Such altitude is kind of exploitation. It seems like you come to God only to receive something and then disappear. With this kind of altitude, you find people who become serious with Christ only during the period of crisis. However, if you don't stay in Christ, you'll remain in crisis.

## FAMILY VALUES

So, if we must change from story to glory and from glory to glory husband and wife we need to start sitting down and start looking at our life and evaluating our resources, evaluating our past and our future together, we need to start doing something about the void that this generation is creating and then the intention to set us apart what are we going to do to pull it together? You may ask yourself this question what are your proof of your connection? How connected are you to the father, God? What are the things you can point to and say that I am connected to my heavenly father?

So, "what is the key to truly knowing God?" First, it is imperative to understand that man, on his own, is incapable of truly knowing God because of man's sinfulness. The Scriptures reveal to us that we are all sinful (Romans 3) and that we fall well short of the standard of holiness required to commune with God. We are also told that the consequence of our sin is death (Romans 6:23) and that we will perish eternally without God unless we accept and receive the promise of Jesus' sacrifice on the cross. So, in order to truly know God, we must first receive Him into our lives. "As many as received Him, to them He gave the right to become children of God, even to those who believe in His name" (John 1:12). Nothing is of greater importance than understanding this truth when it comes to knowing God. Jesus makes it clear that He alone is the way to heaven and to a personal knowledge of God: "I am the way, and the truth, and the life; no one comes to the Father, but through Me" (John 14:6).

There is no requirement to begin this journey besides accepting and receiving the promises mentioned above. Jesus came to breathe life into us by offering Himself as a sacrifice so our sins will not prevent us from knowing God. Once we have received this truth, we can begin the journey of knowing God in a personal way. One of the key ingredients in this journey is understanding that the Bible is God's Word and is His revelation of Himself, His promises, His will. The Bible is essentially a love letter written to us from a loving God who created us to know Him intimately. What better way to learn about our Creator than to immerse ourselves in His Word, revealed to us for this very reason? And it is important to continue this process throughout the entire journey. Paul writes to Timothy, "But as for you, continue in what you have learned and have become convinced of, because you know those from whom you learned it, and how from infancy you have known the Holy Scriptures, which are able to make you wise for salvation through faith in Christ Jesus. All Scripture is God-breathed and is useful for teaching, rebuking, correcting and training in righteousness, so that the man of God may be thoroughly equipped for every good work" (2 Timothy 3:14-16).

Jesus said my sheep know my voice. What are the proofs of your connection to him, how many houses have you bought if that's your proof of connectivity? How many people have you brought to the church, how many people have you prayed for?

How many people have you brought to Christ?

When I take a look at the number of disciples that I mentored and those that flow me, I know that I am connected somehow because I am doing what He has called me to do. This to me is somehow, a personal evaluation and self-examination. I am convinced that I am on track and my inner man also assured me that I am going somewhere. The same can be true with you. You can take a look at some aspect of your life and examine yourself through those things. For example, you won't stay in the same business for years if that business has no prospect of making a profit in the future. Personality, you won't need the Holy Ghost to tell you to quit such business. You will obviously quit and look for something profitable. Don't tell me it was God that sent you there because God won't send you to such a thing that has no future.

## WHAT ARE THE REASONS FOR YOUR DISCONNECTION FROM HIM?

Once again, I am challenging and encouraging you to take action, do something that will put a value to your life. Do something that will keep a mark in this generation. Do something that the world would remember. Do something that will help eradicate the stupendous character the devils and his cohort has implanted in the life of the young ones in this generation. Do something that will have a generational influence and impact. for that is exactly what God wants. He wants you to be remembered forever. He wants you to live a meaningful life.

*"After David had served his generation according to the will of God, he died" (Acts 13:36 NLT).*

My life verse is Acts 13:36, where we're told David is purpose-driven.

Imagine having that statement inscribed on your tombstone: "He served God's purpose in his own generation!" "She served

God's purpose in her own generation!" In my opinion, you could receive no greater honor than that.

So how do you do that?

*"He served God's purpose…"*

God's purpose for you is to use your life in worship, ministry, evangelism, discipleship, and fellowship. The Church allows us to do it together. We are not alone in serving him.

*"…In his own generation."*

The truth is you can't serve God in any other generation except your own! You may want to—but it's only wishful thinking. We cannot bring back the past. Whether we like it or not, we must minister to people in the culture as it really is—not in some past form that we may have idolized in our minds.

You don't know the final chapter of your life, but you can be confident of this: "… that he who began a good work in you will carry it on to completion until the day of Christ Jesus" (Phil. 1:6 NIV).

God finishes whatever he starts. He is Alpha and Omega, the beginning and the end. There are many factors that influence your life, things you have no control over: your background, nationality, age, giftedness. These were determined by the sovereignty of God.

But there is one important factor that you do have a control over: how much you choose to believe God as you serve your generation according to his will.

# CHAPTER 5

# RECONNECTING THE DISCONNECTED

L et us look at a few definitions. The word reconnects – reconnecting the disconnected generation – reconnect is, "to join" or "to link" or "to fasten together".

To reconnect means that something has happened to disconnect us and whatever it was, we are sorting it out. We are creating a joining together and we are refastening what has loosed together again. Before you read further, "I want to prophesy to you, that every way you have been disconnected from your creator, I see you being reconnected in the name of Jesus". I see whatever has loosened in your lives, relationship and families being reconnected together in the name of Jesus. Every way that you have been disconnected from God in your prayer life, in fasting, in your spiritual obligation, in your giving, in your commitment to God and to your personal values that makes God endorses you, I see you reconnecting in the mighty name of Jesus.

## MARRIAGE, THE GOVERNMENT, AND THE CHURCH

To reconnect with someone, you have to build a bridge. The church, for example, is a bridge to connect to God. A marriage or a home is also a bridge to reconnect back to God because in the beginning God created you male and female and in connecting man back to himself in the original state, God said to multiply. The Government you have today is one of the three things God instituted Himself - which are Marriage, Government, and the church.

**Marriage** – God observed that it was not good for man to be alone, so He brought the woman out of man and marriage became institutionalized.

**The Government** – God said let them rule over and have dominion upon everything on earth – that was government

**Church** – The bible said that God came down and visited them. He said where two or three meets together in my name, there I will be in the midst of them.

Those three institutions were created by God Himself and they are a bridge of connection between us and God. This was why when the Bible was describing Jesus as the Messiah who was to come; it said Government shall be upon His shoulder. Therefore, the governments of this world are to be ruled as a bridge or intermediary to connect people to God and this was why the first government that was had to wait for God to appoint them a king.

The first type of government anywhere on earth was a Theocracy. The Government of God for the people to establish a bridge between the people and God – a channel of communication with God. So, when I am kneeling down to pray or reading His words, I am communicating with Him. When I was reading a letter or email from my wife, I was connecting with her even though she was in another country this implies that When you are reading the Word of God, you're connecting with God. When you pay your taxes and National Insurance to the Treasury, what you're doing is, you're connecting with the government. When you pay your offerings and tithes, what you are doing is that you are connecting with God.

Next, is to associate mentally or emotionally, that is why we can associate or disassociate mentally or emotionally or otherwise. Are you connected with your Creator or who are you disconnected? Ruminate over these questions and answer all that affect you. Are you connected with your spouse or maybe yours is your children, are you connected with your destiny or are you connected with your leaders, your Pastor or are you connected with yourself?

## WHAT DOES IT MEAN TO DISCONNECT?

If to connect means to join, disconnect means to disjoin. Merriam Webster dictionary defines it as "to separate (something) from something else: to break a connection between two or more things"

I prophesy that everything that is disconnecting or disjoining you from God is broken in the name of Jesus. Everything that is disjoining you from your spouse, your children and your destiny, today I decree it is broken in the name of Jesus.

To disconnect also means not coherent, simile irrational. Today you see married couples who were joined together in holy matrimony, are in a jeopardy of disconnection. The same man and woman you pursued and pursued and that you will kill yourself if you were not married to him or her; the same person that when coming to visit, it was like heaven was coming to the earth and now coming in and you are behaving as if he or she is not there. This is what disconnection means.

The same person you were writing on his or her wall for the

whole world to see and read as your lover, your mentor, your honey and the sugar in your tea. the same person that if anyone could say you should not marry you would have said no – you shall kill yourself because he/she is the only man on earth, now all of a sudden there is a disjoint or a disconnect. My prayer for you reading this book is that God would help you develop godly values that will cause you to look at your spouse and see Love in personify. I pray that this love will come upon you in that way that you'll see your spouse and renew your vows and value for him daily.

To the glory of God, I and my wife have been married for ten years now and no qualms. We enjoy the beauty of love and experience the real love that dissolves any iota of confusion and hypocrisy in our relationship. We have a stress-free marriage and the devil himself can testify that we are untouchable. As a matter of fact, and as a sign of love, we renewed our vows during our 10th anniversary which was on the 20th of July 2014 and reconnected ourselves, after which we went for a honeymoon as if we just got married. Love, love, love! That's it! Marriage is an inseparable and irrevocable union between two people including God as the supreme being in it. Nothing can separate us! We're bound and bonded for life! No devil can try to separate us.

## MARRIAGE

Marriage is a union that determines the impact and the foundation of a nation. This was what said through James draw to me and I shall draw near to you.

*"Come near to God and he will come near to you"* (James 4:8a NIV)

We are more privilege in this generation than the generation before us, we see more technological advancement than the previous generation. In the last sixty years, this generation has seen more advancement upon advancement in almost every sphere of life. The television, for example, came into existence in the late 1920s by Scottish inventor John Loggie Baird and by Match 25, 1925 the first motion image came into existence. Since then we have been having more technological advancement over and over again. The generation before us has no such privilege to see them on screen. All they had was pictures.

Moreover, in those days when they took photograph, they have a waiting time of up to three weeks before they can see a clear picture and later on the process was developed and the waiting time for the clear picture was reduced due to technological advancement. Then we have the arrival of Polaroid camera which made the photograph instant. We have come a long way, there are some certain inventions that have not been made popularize yet and most people in this generation are not aware of it. Now in the comfort of our sitting room or at your convenience, we can use our phones to snap pictures, look at it on the screen and if we do not like it you can delete it and if we like it, we can have it published in seconds for the whole world to see.

During those days what you see is what you get. Those days you have to dress up, make an effort to take yourself to the photographer because not everyone could afford a camera or even to hire a photographer. In those days the camera was so big that you need a horse carriage to carry them. When the camera first arrived in Africa, people bow down and worshipped the camera and the photographer. Not just in Africa that this happened, including some Asian countries but Africans took it to the extreme that as men began to multiply upon the surface of the earth people began to see wonders and as they see them, they began to marvel and worship these God's wonders.

For instance, when the sun came up, they worship it, believing it to be a supernatural thing lighten their life and they worship the

Sun; the moon came out, they marvel and began to worship the moon – so we have the sun worshiper, moon worshipers, when they saw the wave of the sea and they worship the sea and up to date in some religion have the god of the sun, god of the moon, god of the rain, etc. What does it really mean to worship God? Are we to worship him by worship a thing, or is worship a song, a style, a nice voice? What really is worship?

# CHAPTER 6

# THE ART OF WORSHIP

People have some time be disconnected from the real purpose of worship. I will recommend you reading this book to read the by Dr. Myles Munroe called The Purpose and Power of Praise & Worship. Worship isn't a song, worship is fellowship. It is also connected to word koinonia in Greek which means communion and also means fellowship. It is a kind of intimate relationship with the Maker of the universe, The alpha, and the omega. It is a relationship that transforms you as you communicate with the Supreme Being Jehovah Yahweh.

You can't correctly worship God and your life remains the same. No, Never! It is like you get into a room packed full and clouded with perfume and you expect you come out without the flavor over your life. Nope! When you get in such atmosphere you will come out with a good smelling ornament of flavor and everyone around you will know that you came from a chamber full of flavor. That is how worship is, it transforms you and the more you get into such atmosphere you find yourself communing deeper and deeper and deeper like deep calleth unto deep. In the old testament of the bible, such atmosphere was mostly described as upper room, inner core, outermost part, the inner chamber, holy of holies, etc. There were all areas that you couldn't go in and come back the same, something had to happen to you. Some people get in there and were transformed, others became deaf and dump, other died, others weren't permitted to get in until they were clean.

So, in the nutshell, it is an intimate relationship that transforms the worshiper into something supernaturally great. If this generation becomes a generation of praise and worship, believe you me, our society and nations will feel the tremendous impact of this. We have problem reconnection people that are disconnected. By talking to disconnected generation, we would instantly get them hook to the source of life as a result of that good smelling flavor that rooms around us.

God is worship and we are created as human beings to worship God. Man is created for one reason only that reason to worship God. We are created for one intention of the creator God, that is to fulfill His will on earth and that is to worship Him. In my native language, that is the Yoruba language to worship something is to "bo" and when you are "worshipping" something you do it with everything you have, body, soul, and spirit. Those people who mostly worship idols, mostly wake up very early in the morning and religiously reference it. They will pour oil on it, sing praise to it, dance and pay obeisance every morning with all their heart and all their mind. They worship things which cannot respond to their cry but till they devote all their time and energy to it by giving it everything they have got.

However, God worshipers nowadays that is those who worship the real God on the other hand show some level of seriousness and hypocrisy. Some are experts at what is wrong, such people come to church only to see and identify what is wrong with everybody else or what is not going right in the church service. They become an expert in gossips and complain about everything in the church;" You see they could have put that thing there or that pastor or this pastor can speak better he should have been given the microphone." Such people haven't come to worship because when we come to worship, our heart and our whole being should have been immersed in the worship. Those idol worshipers I am referring to worship without microphones, they worship without drums, they worshiped without piano but they used their mouths to make music with which they worship their idols in rhythmical sounds, they get so immersed in their worship to the point they got intoxicated. They even create resonant with which they worship. They raised the tempo to the point where they begin to chant and hollow – that is the way a devoted worshipper should do. Sometimes our dressing repels people from God rather than propelling them to Him. Putting on skirts and attire that makes it difficult for one to differentiate you from prostitutes in the streets isn't a good thing to do. This is a kind of an abominable art that shows that one has been discounted from His Creator. We must always realize that worshipping God is not only doe by singing or dancing it goes beyond that it's our way of life. We must strive to worship God in all our doings.

The Israelites needed a deliverance from Egypt and God heard their cry and set them free and let them loose. When God said they should go out, God told them to go to their neighbors, their employers, their slave masters and ask them for anything they wanted; they were asked to take their gold, their silver. So, they went to the Egyptians and whatever they asked the Egyptians they received. Just a few miles down the road, the Lord asked their leader Moses to come and wait upon Him for a hearing on the mountain, while Moses was on the mountain with God, they turned against God and started worshipping Idols that is the very same thing God has blessed them with from the Egyptians; the Gold etc. was blended and an idol was formed.

## CREATE A POSITIVE ENVIRONMENT

Sometimes the job that God gave to us for livelihood is what we worship as mammon, remember you can't serve God and mammon at the same time. You've to make choice. You're either for God or for mammon, either for GOD or for Gold. I urge you to trip off every heaven weight and burden that want to take you off, God. As a child of this peculiar and royal generation of God, I encourage you to take bold steps that will enable you to walk with God and fulfill your life calling and purpose. Create the right environment for yourself. Trip yourself off friends who are taking you backward. Connect with the right people and thus life would become easy and enjoyable for you. Why do I say you should create the right environment for yourself? This is because it has been proven that environment determines about 40% of our success and growth in life. You can't determine to be like a lion and you walk with goats. A lion walks with lions. If you want to be like a lion you have to walk with a lion, talk with lions' fellowship with lions and thereby you will see yourself becoming a lion and thinking lion a lion. Saul became a prophet by being in the company of prophets! Associates determine your success, therefore look for the right association for yourself.

It has been said that it is a wise man or woman who lives life by "majoring on the majors" instead of "majoring on the minors." But to do that, you and I must be able to figure out what things in life are major, what things are truly important, and what things are trivial or nonessential.

One way to discover what is "major" is to find out what is important to God, to determine what it is that He attaches special significance to. And in Scripture, He does give us a clue.

"Associate with men of good quality if you esteem your own reputation; for it is better to be alone than in bad company.' George Washington

Following with the Holy Spirit is a kind of associate with God. It brings down the presence of God in everything you do. When you learn to grow with God, you become transformed into the image of God and thereby beginning the real person he has created you to be. A refuted generation is the generation that has disconnected himself completely from the presence of God. Such generations become self-center center rather than God center. Some of us we worship the life God has given us that we began to worship ourselves. Most people who are consumed by themselves focused their entire life on how to please their external environment, and on how to make themselves more attractive than on how to attract the presence and the glory of God. When God called you a royal priesthood, a peculiar person, and a chosen generation, he knows what he meant and truly he meant what he said. However, this won't happen automatically! You have to align your ways to His way in order to fully grabs what he has in store for you. His Words are the roadmaps to the pathway of greatness and to the life he has prepared for you.

Some of us still experience things difficulties, that is things aren't going the way we desire, it might seem like God is no longer a good God but God is calling us to draw near to and he shall draw near to you. I have been serving God for a while and I know what being disconnected from God is. Anyone disconnected from God is like a fish taken out of the water, I know what fullness of God is and I know what emptiness of God is. I know when you are empty and I know when you are full. If you have enjoyed the presence of God before you know that when you don't have His divine presence you are not happy on the inside. It is only a carnal person that is pleased with the state of carnality. If you are truly connected to God, when you are not connected you will be uncomfortable, so be comfortable with the state of sin means that you are not yet a child of God. If I do not call my mum after a while I feel guilty so is the same if you don't pray you become a prey.

If you do not pray for a year, two years, one month, two months and you feel comfortable then something must be wrong with you, you are surely not a child of God. If you are in the house of God and you are happy to be a spectator rather than been a worshiper then you need to ask yourself whether you are really a child of GOD. I need you to understand something, my father builds properties and sometimes it takes me a while to visit these properties but when I go there one of the things I do is when I noticed what is wrong, I do not criticize it or say who did this or that. This is one of the things you do when you are divinely connected – my father, for example, is no more but I have decided is to know what needs fixing, and how much it is going to cost to put it right, how much for that roof, the gate, because when you are a son, you are part of the fixer. You are the solution and not part of the problem when you are a child of God and you walk on the street and you see people who are not safe you cannot be happy inside of you.

My son once asked me a question – he asked have we fed our fish? We have well over fifty fish in the aquarium and we have forgotten to feed them. So, I said what happens if we go on holiday, does it mean the fish will feed them? so my son replies and said maybe the fish too should go on holidays that means they have to jump out of the water and so on. I said immediately the fish would be out of the water, it will stop to be a fish, it becomes a prey and lose its entire life. The same way many of us think we can just walk out on God, the fact is you can't go on holiday to God because no matter where you are He is there before you. You are with Him – but you cannot be in this world or this earth and not be connected with God your maker, you cannot be on this earth and not be incongruent with your maker. You cannot be on this earth and not be in communication with your maker. If you are not deaf and not dump, you will speak to the one who made you. Everything that is worship always requires a way in which it should be worshipped. Those who worship inanimate object create a way and manner in which they will worship it. You see? Our God said those who must worship Him must worship or must do so in spirit and in truth – in another word, it is a spirituality that authenticates connectivity that is the only way you can validate your relationship with God.

Connectivity is a spiritual thing so being connected or when you are connected is through your spirit. Your body will decay, your body will disconnect one day, your body is a suit that one day will die and be buried and will turn back into the soil. Worms will eat up this flesh on the day. The only thing that is making the worms not to eat up the flesh of the body at the moment is blood. This was why the capital punishment God meted out Herod was his body was being eaten alive by worms. God showed him that this body just suits. Disconnection with God is so risky. Risky in the sense that your spirit becomes inactive because you are essentially a spirit that has a soul and it lives in a body. Many people are only carrying their soul in their body, they have never discovered their spirit and many people will die never fully realize the treasure that lies in their spirit.

On the other hand, there are those who are so curious to tap into the spiritual realm and in doing so they are instead using their mind to become spiritual. Well, this is an erroneous doctrine and the reason why we have several religious sects. You can't use your soul to tap into the realm of God, rather you have to use your spirit to realize the fullness of God. God is spirit and anyone that has to chat with must do so in the realm in of the spirit and not with the brain. Your soul is the emotional, intellectual aspect of man. It's not your intellect that communicates with him rather it is your spirit. Trying to search for God using brains is the reason why there is all kind of religions and people carry out all sort of experiment to achieve their quest. They are looking for something which they themselves can't tell and it only exists in their mind, that's a myth.

The Bible says very clearly that you were created for connections. Life is all about connections!

"… Listen, all you people… The Lord will stay with you as long as you stay with him! If you seek him, you will find him. But if you abandon him, he will abandon you…For a long time, Israel had been without the true God… and without God's law. But in their distress, they turned to the Lord and sought him

"God has given you one face, and you make yourself another."
—William Shakespeare

Spirit is not physically tangible but is more evidence that the physical the same way oxygen is not physically tangible but you have tubes that you can use to see oxygen. According to the universal law of vibration, it starts that everything around us vibrates even the solid substance you might see around you; It all vibrates at a particular frequency. It also states that the same principles apply to our physical world when it comes to thoughts, feelings, desires, and wills in the Etheric world. Matters such as sound, thing, even though has its own unique vibrational frequency. However, it looks like we are separated but according to physics, we are not because we are all connected at a particular lowest level. Science, however, has explained this in details using unified field theory and quantum physics.

Similarly, there are angels and spirits that are gathered or worshipping with us every time we gather be it as a church or individually. The scripture noted that the angels of God encamp round about them that fear him. So, if you cannot see them where you're right just know within your spirit that they are there with you. Perhaps you can also pray like Elisha prayed for God to open the eyes of his servant to see that those that were with them were more than the armies that surrounded them (2 Kings 6:17). You won't need me to still tell how many thousands of angels are with you right now. Do you know how many? My friend, there are thousands however your faith or level of belief can limit them. It can limit your exploration of their present. Now you see what God has given to this generation and dispensation? Thousands of Angels to surround us wherever we go. The corruptness and the pervertness of this generation would only limit the influence of angelic manifestation in our life, nations, and generation. My prayer is, that will not be your case in Jesus name.

Though we cannot see them with our naked eyes, God is wherever two or three gathered together in His name and all the time God is there. That is why you see some people as soon as they come into the church they just go on their knees and start thanking God and praising for everything He has done in their life. They offered fervent prayers and thanksgivings to God for what He has done. Sometimes, I look at myself in the mirror and I just say thank you, Jesus, thank him for my family, for the church and for all that is happening around me. I know that He lives in the inside of me all the time and I can chat with Him at any time. The least that I can say is Father I just thank you and glory to your name... Hallelujah, thank you, glory to your name, Hallelujah thank you. At least you are assured you are speaking to the one in the inside of you. Let me say this to you reading this book, never live a prayerless life; Man is a tripartite being and a lot of people would be shocked when they would realize only at the dead that their spirit is different from their body. The first time some people will have an encounter with their spirit is when they are dead and all of a sudden, they would now know that the spirit world is real.

## THE GRACEFUL GOD

Now the bible says God is a spirit and those who must worship Him must worship Him in spirit and in truth. This is one of our principal text in this book!

*"God is a spirit, and his worshipers must worship in the Spirit and in truth." (John 4:24)*

If God is a spirit, my spirit that came out of God must always be connected to the spirit of God. He is the source of life. Whenever my spirit connects with him, it gets a life and gets it more abundantly. Whenever God sees that men are disconnected. He cries out loud and says "draw near unto me, and I shall draw near unto you." In Isaiah 1:18 He said "come now and let us reason together" saith God "though your sins are as scarlet they shall be white as snow; though they be red as crimson, they shall be as wool." Do you know man's spirit is still able to connect with God even in the place of sin? God said come unto me though your sins are many, they shall be wiped off and you shall be whiter than snow. Wow! What a graceful and merciful God. You can see the reason while the devil short many people off from following God. The devil will hardly remind you of that rather he will remind you of your sins – that is why the Bible called him the accuser of the brethren. He makes you think you have no access to God because of what you have done wrong, this is why God is calling you here, saying to you "come even if your sin is scarlet, He said come they shall be as white as snow."

Somebody once said to me, "Pastor Great, I really want to give my life to Jesus, but you see I really have this weakness, I go out and I drink, fornicate etc." I simply reply and said well,

64

if you are waiting for that to change before you give your life to Jesus you will never give it because you have no capacity within yourself to give it up by yourself, you're to surrender to him so he will help you take the burden away by his grace that will be impacted upon you, you'll be able to overcome future challenges. You see it is He the creator that has the capacity to repair, fix what He has created, it is He who has the spare part to repair what He has manufactured because He is the creator. Then I later asked the person a question, I said; "do you think those who are born again do not sin?" Does this mean that people coming to the church, such as people doing fraud, adultery, fornication, gamblers, etc? Does it mean that they are all pure? Nope! We all come to him with our weaknesses and flaws to find grace to help in time of troubles. we all are in church to find grace to remain connected to him, that is why we go to him. Not because we are clean but because we are unclean, not because we're perfect but because we need perfectness, not because we're powerful but rather because we're weak and we need strength. Hallelujah! No matter your weakness, just come to him as you are. Don't try to think about how you're going to change; No! For your reasoning and imagination would rather weigh you down, simply come the way you are.

Though we put suits, we all put on our head gear, wear beautiful attires and we wear makeup, doesn't actually mean that we are flawless. You can't tell what everyone goes through only if they open up their own life to you. We are to see everyone as God sees them. We can't condemn anyone for only the devil condemns and accused. Now if you think your worship is accepted what makes you think my own worship will not be accepted. He invited us all to come as we are, FOR HE WILL MAKE US WHITER THAN SNOW. This is the only way we can rebuild a disconnected generation.

As a matter of fact, he said while we all yet sinners He died for us. The principal reason why so many people are disconnected is they think and see only imperfection, some people also leave their job, their marriage, some even walk out of the church because they see imperfection. Imperfection is not a proof that God is absent rather it is a proof that God's presence and also that you need Him. It is a proof that God is present because everywhere you see God at work, you will also see the devil trying to counterfeit Him.

## THE GATHERING OF THE SAINTS
*"One day the angels came to present themselves before the Lord and Satan also came with them." (Job 1:6)*

Anywhere you see the work of God going on, the devil will also be there wanting to attack. Everywhere you see the work of God going great or something great is happening to you or maybe in your marriage, you'll also see the-the devil trying to attack. When that happened, never lose hope, just know that God is on your side. If you are in the camp of the devil there is no need for him to attack you because nobody likes to score his own goal. Why would someone attack what is already his? Rather he will make them an instrument of his use. When you are in the camp, the only reason the devil will definitely not attack you is when you decide to tend toward the Light and be connected to Him

In this life, words exist on opposite sides. The devil is on the other side and is always trying to antagonize whatever God is doing. Whenever he sees a glorious future and he will sit down and begin to bring sickness, diseases, bring oppression and begin to plant destruction for the person. When he sees a bright and glorious child and he will begin to put stubbornness in the child straight away; When he sees a great marriage, that has got a brighter future from the wedding day, he starts to put discord between husband and wife and caused them to be unable to do great things. So, such couples spend the bulk of their life never understanding each other but a connection with their divine source will show them that in the beginning, it was not like this, for there is still Hope. Great future attracts greater distraction, the new level new devil. No change No challenge!

Until there is progress on the way that is when you will see oppression. No matter the situation is hope and there is always a breakthrough. However, for you to get this breakthrough, you have to step some conscious decision. You have to make this conscious decision by saying, Lord I am connected with you, I am divinely connected with you, my life is in your hand –

He said "come near to me and I will draw near to you, draw near" Say this to yourself with boldness and say "If I draw near to him, He will draw near to me". Great!

*But you have come to Mount Zion, to the city of the living God, the heavenly Jerusalem. You have come to thousands upon thousands of angels in joyful assembly." (Hebrews 12:22 NIV)*

As earlier said, when you gather as a group or individually and in the name of the Lord, you have heavenly backing and support. In the heavenly realm, you're connected with an innumerable company of angels. Therefore, if God is true with us he doesn't come alone, He comes with the host of angels. I love the way the-the Igbo language put it. They call it "Odogunna dike a" which means a man of war and His appearance is terrible. The bible says, mountains skip when he comes. When the Queen is coming to a place or city, she sends an envoy into that town and the whole area will be filled security officers everywhere. You will see police riders, cars and other entourages – tens and hundreds of police officers on that street. That's same way God does it, but greater than the queen of England or anyone on Earth. God can't show up without the tremendous power in place. You see the above verse says you have come to Mount Zion – which is the Church, you have come to mount Zion the city of the living God, the heavenly Jerusalem and to the innumerable company of the angels. Whenever we gather as a church, we don't gather alone, we gather with the host of angels and we become divinely connected.

# CHAPTER 7

# THE POWER OF THE WORD

One time, someone brought their child to our ministry, when we just started the church a few years ago and child used to faint, or with convulsion. The child came into the choir the first week and he fainted. They called an ambulance and two weeks later, the child came into the choir again and fainted. The choir members wanted to call the ambulance again, I said no, don't call an ambulance. The father of the child looked at me and said: "my child is fainting and you said we shouldn't call an ambulance?" I said "no don't call an ambulance it is an abuse on God if she is serving God at this altar and then God must heal her. And immediately, I said whatever it is that wanted to take her, can't tamper in this place. I said don't call an ambulance, but the man went ahead to call the ambulance and before the paramedics and the ambulance arrived the child has recovered and gone back singing in the choir. Now, since that day till today, the girl has never fainted again. Some people come to the opinion that I Pastor Great is powerful. Well, it is not Pastor Great that is powerful, it is the presence of the highest God that is powerful.

We cannot be in the presence of God and natural or supernatural healing won't take place. Supernatural miracles are not our abilities, it is God's ability and he does it as He wishes. However, healing and miracles are His will. Therefore, be rest assured that miracle is certain! Hallelujah. This is what I struggle with when some ministers make supernatural occurrences and miracles the anchor of their ministries. The miracle is man's interpretation of God's common sense. Whatever miracle you need is taking place right now as you are reading this book. You cannot be reading this book with expectation and wanting God to touch you, and then He does not. No, Impossible! The woman with the issue of blood got healed by simply touching Jesus' garment. Jesus did not say how many of you have the issue of blood come and I will heal you. No, He simply came in and His presence and even shadow did the work. Now you see, the woman with the issue of blood understood what she wanted and went to him and Jesus said: "someone has touched me, somebody drew virtue".

As you keep reading, I know you're drawing virtues for your healing and miracles. You know, healing is the children's bread. Therefore, you have the audacity and legal right to be healed. Confess boldly to yourself "this situation in my life I join up with the innumerable number of angels and declare I am healed in Jesus' name". As you speak out loud, you can see the healing and change taking place right now. It is a conscious decision that we have to make in your life that you're going to receive your miracles and never to base your life on miracle alone but rather on the Word of God. You are going to be firmly founded on the Word of God and whatever the word cannot do, you do not want it done. If God cannot increase you, you don't want the growth by your strength, it is God that works in us both to will and to do. Just watch what God is going to do to you and boldly confess that God is more than enough.

If you are divinely connected, just watch what God is doing, you'll have a continuous stream of miracle flowing in your life. Reconnect yourself in every way you have disconnected yourself. You may have come reading this book to fulfill your religious rites or for reading sake, etc., but, I challenge you today, just begin to reconnect yourself to him. Endeavor to stay connected with your maker and in your heart just begin to say to him - Lord I need more of you and more than words could say and I need you more. I need to know you more and to understand that you live on the inside of me. Be aware that God is seated right where you are and that He lives in you. Be aware that the more of His word you read the more of Him you have on the inside of you.

*Let the word of Christ dwell in you richly in all wisdom; teaching and admonishing one another in psalms and hymns and spiritual songs, singing with grace in your hearts to the Lord" (KJV) (Colo 3:16)*

He said let the Word of Christ dwell in you richly. Richly he said, and in all wisdom. In Ecclesiastes, it shows the consequences of disconnection, Ecclesiastes 5:6

*"Do not let your mouth lead you into sin. And do not protest to the temple messenger, "My vow was a mistake." Why should God be angry at what you say and destroy the work of your hands?" (NIV),*

What the Bible is saying here is when you are unconscious that you are a spirit, the spirits around you, begin to take advantage of you by collecting what messages you are passing on to them via negative confession. You need to watch what word comes out of your mouth for there is power in your words. What you say is what you get and it becomes what you attract. In the new age, it is called the law of attraction. Anyone confessing negative things will keep attracting negativity. There is no way negative is going to become positive when you keep on confessing only negative words. Negativity attracts negativity~! For everybody likes to be in the same family of harmony and birds of the same feathers

71

flock together. King Solomon said 'He that Walk with the wise and become wise, for a companion of fools suffers harm'". In other words, it says "Show me your friends, I'll show you your future."

If you keep being negative, you will be composed of a bundle of negative energy all around your life. Even those who come near you might be affected by your negativity. It will only take grace and they're conscious for them not to be influenced by the negative forces around you. Negativity has a negative multiplier effect on our environment and our society. If all you are doing is tearing, tearing and tearing, I am afraid, you're heading toward danger. You can't be saying "we can't afford it, I don't know, how we can do it, etc." if that is your statement all the time, that is how your life is going to be. Only those who believe they can, can really can, but those who believe they cannot; cannot. Life is a matter of choice. It gives you what you say, the scripture says don't say before an angel it is an error.

When you say you are sick, how can you be sick? because you are disconnected without realizing that there is healing and the Healer. He who created you can fix whatever is wrong with your health and your life. I like given this illustration from my father in the Lord; If I give you a bible as a gift, I cannot take it back because it's not any longer mine but yours. Do I have it? How can I have if I have given it to you. So, if something is given to someone, it is given and it no longer with the giver. So, the scripture said in the book of Isaiah that He himself took our infirmity, He bore all our sickness. It says the chastisement of our peace was upon Him and by stripe, we are healed. Therefore, He has taken away my sickness and diseases, it's no longer mine. Now, I have evidence that I cannot have what He has already taken on my behalf. If there is a headache - you cannot have it because he has already taken it on your behalf. You can feel it, it might be present, but you don't have it because He took it away. Hallelujah!

If you are consciously connected, you will know that you cannot have it. Some people go to the extent of saying I have a backache and some saying this "my sickness"; you even personalized it by saying "my". Oh No! you have personalized the problem because you have not seen the existence of the Creator, the healer. The one who is the healer said you have overcome, but you can only overcome sickness and another infirmity with your heart, mind and your mouth. That is why the bible says confession of the mouth made unto salvation. It is the decision of the mouth that follows the expression of the heart.

*"The word is near you; it is in your mouth and in your heart,] that is, the message concerning faith that we proclaim: If you declare with your mouth, "Jesus is Lord," and believe in your heart that God raised him from the dead, you will be saved. 10 For it is with your heart that you believe and is justified, and it is with your mouth that you profess your faith and are saved. (NIV) (Romans 10:8-10)*

It means the Word of faith is written even in the mouth – the word salvation is the word – sozo- which means deliverance, prosperity. If you are poor, your salvation is riches or provision, if you are sick, your salvation is full health. If for example, someone is drowning, you say someone should save him/her. Salvation does not only mean to surrender your life to Jesus Christ. Salvation is to be translated from which any uncomfortable state into another comfort stage for which the Holy Spirit is the chief comforter. If you need a better state, from any condition in another word you need salvation. Salvation is a translation from unrighteousness into righteousness.

If you are connected with God your spirit will work in faith even if you are still doing that which you ought not to do. In your heart you believe that I am the righteousness of God and with your mouth you confess it that I am coming out of this, my life is better than this, I am going to work it all out, devil I am going to staple all over you and I will have victory and power over this. And so, shall it be! The flesh is always in contention and in constant temptation. Even Pope and Bishops are visited every day by the flesh. Don't think you are the only one the devil is tempting. You're not the only one, for as long as you are still on earth he will be around.

# CHAPTER 8

# FALSE SENSE OF INTIMACY

False sense of intimacy is the reason why many Christians remain shallow and immature and what do I mean by false sense of intimacy – many people come to church and before the worship starts they are just spectators but once the music goes on and it is a song they like and are familiar with, you now see them crying and crying as if someone turns the switch of their life on. Like when they sing "Lord I give you my heart, I give you my soul I live for you alone" Tears will be rolling down their eyes like someone open the tap, it is a false sense of intimacy. They are connected to the music and not the Lord they came to adore. Worship is not music nor is it a song. It is a relationship which is not triggered by anything but by love. This is a false sense of intimacy God alone knows those who are connected with him.

Let me share with you a story the first time I enter Europe that was in the UK, I had a false sense of identity because I have been dreaming about coming to Europe for almost fourteen Year. I had an expensive phone that was given to me by a friend, it was one of the most expensive Motorola phone at that point in time. Phones were still regarded as a luxury and weren't popular by then. This was my first week in the UK; I went to Victoria Line and while on the underground, and I went on the phone I started walking alone because I wanted everyone to notice me and see me talking on the phone as a "big man". Where I came from in Africa by then, mobile phones were a big deal. It was only for the big guys in town and having a phone was like you have arrived! so I went on the phone, I started shouting "Hello, Hello, hello!!!" Talking to myself with an imaginary communicator, a business partner. I told him that I would transport three container loads of some imaginary stuff to him in two weeks' time. I was inviting someone else to come and see me in my office to collect a cheque. I was feeling good having conversation on the underground. As soon as we got to Waltham stone, a young beautiful Spanish lady walked up to me with confidence and say to me, "I am just curious and just wanted to know; because we were all looking at you that you are either mad or a terrorist, in case there is a third option, what network are you using?" I asked her what do you mean. She said you were using your phone on the underground, I stared at her and she further said phones don't work on the underground, so I quickly say thank you my sister and I vanished.

What an illusion? Living an illusionary life is dangerous as living in hell. It is the same way many of us live. We live our life to please someone who doesn't even notice us. We dress to please people who don't even care about us. When you are not connected, your life becomes like a royal that is driven by someone else.

True intimacy with God is something that has been sought by Christians since Christ walked the earth. It is natural for Christians to long to experience the closeness of an intimate relationship with God. But true intimacy with God is not simply a feeling on a par with a romantic relationship. It goes much deeper than emotion, down to our very souls and reflected by our actions.

"For the LORD detests the perverse but takes the upright into his confidence" (Proverbs 3:32). God cannot have an intimacy with evil or with disobedient Christians. True intimacy with God begins with drawing near to Him. God in his loving kindness will draw near everyone who seeks him deligently in truth and righteousness "Draw near to God, and he will draw near to you. Cleanse your hands, you sinners, and purify your hearts, you double-minded" (James 4:8). Certainly, God will never draw near in intimacy with the unrighteous, but those who have been cleansed by the blood of Christ and have received His righteousness at the cross (2 Corinthians 5:21) have the hope of intimacy with God. In fact, it is only those who have been saved by grace through faith (Ephesians 2:8–9) who have that hope, because Christ is the hope through which we draw near to God (Hebrews 7:19).

Jesus is, in fact, the model of intimacy with God because He and the Father are one (John 10:30), and no relationship can be closer than that oneness with the Father that Jesus experienced. His relationship with the Father was characterized by love and obedience. In love, Jesus came to earth to do His Father's will. He did nothing on His own, but in all things did the will of His Father (John 5:30). This was most evident in the Garden of Gethsemane the night before His crucifixion. Suffering the agony of anticipating what was to come, Jesus asked that the fate He was about to suffer might be removed from Him, but He ended the plea by saying, "Yet not My will, but Yours be done" (Luke 22:42). Here we see a perfect example of true intimacy reflected in obedience as Jesus yielded His will to that of His Father.

"Clothing and makeup and hair and all of that so much indicates the kind of person you are inside and the person you are presenting on the outside. Sometimes they are in conflict, and sometimes they are the same. That psychology of the exterior informing the interior is just so interesting." Tatiana Maslany

# CHAPTER 9

# SPIRITUAL OBLIGATIONS

A s you proceed into this chapter of this book, I strongly believe God is speaking to you and you can clearly hear when he's topping you up. Each time you get outside and relate with your immediate environment, you boldly claim to be a Christian which in turn is a false proclamation of identity. If you don't take a conscious and instant decision to be transformed and be connected to God then you are heading to eternal condemnation. If you cannot worship him it automatically means you are not his follower because the bible made it clear that if we must worship him, it must be in truth and spirit.

Christian worship engages both heart and head. It necessitates true doctrine about the Father and his Son, and their partnership in rescuing sinners, and due emotion about that doctrine. It is both an affair of the heart and an affair of the mind. Piper sums it up as "strong affections for God rooted in truth."

Worship must be vital and real in the heart, and worship must rest on a true perception of God. There must be spirit and there must be truth... Truth without emotion produces dead orthodoxy and a church full of artificial admirers... On the other hand, emotion without truth produces empty frenzy and cultivates shallow people who refuse the discipline of rigorous thought. But true worship comes from people who are deeply emotional and who love deep and sound doctrine. Strong affections for God rooted in truth are the bone and marrow of biblical worship. I normally say if you cannot give God your tithe and your offering, which is the cheapest form of expression of love, you cannot love Him.

The scriptures say "For God so loved the world that He gave, and he gave all, the best that He has"; whereas many of us will rationalize giving until dead. Such people will say I don't believe in this. It is just a way the church uses to extort people. let me say something to you, the principle of Tax and National Insurance started from the principles God laid down for man, the only way God wants to fund His kingdom is through tithes and offering. The only way God wants to fund a church that He established is through tight and offering, thus it is a system and ordinances that God had given to Moses. It is the system that the Romans also learned and set up the principles of tax collection. Today before your wages or salaries reaches your hand, they have removed your taxes and National Insurance. What do they use the deduction for in the UK for example; they use it to uphold and maintain the country?

The kingdom of God on earth of which the church is part of is maintained just by you taking that awesome decision saying; Lord, you have given me hundred percent and I am returning ten percent to you so that the work of your ministry can continue and grow to the hearing of those who aren't saved yet. Though giving doesn't end there but it's the principal of all giving because it's clearly stated in the bible. We are instructed to demonstrate the love of God towards our parents, pastors, to the poor, and to all that needed to be supported to bring the salvation of Christ unto them. These and more are different ways we are to show our being connected to him, and all these are called obligations that is spiritual obligations. Attending church is a spiritual obligation, the bible said you "should forsake not the gathering of one another's.

You cannot be spiritual without fulfilling the spiritual obligation. One of the first law or obligation of the spirit is prayer. Jesus was speaking in Luke 18:1- He said "men always ought to pray and never to give up" What is prayer – prayer is communication between man and God or put it this way, prayer is communication between man and deity. So, this is why people pray to Dogs when they made the dog a deity, some pray to cow and all other lifeless creatures by man especially in India, Nepal. The question you are to answer now is, who is your God that you pray to? you ought to have communication with Him on a daily, hourly and second basis. You are dry when you do not have communication with your maker. I pray today that God will divinely connect you as to Him as you read this book in the name of Jesus. Remember, if you don't pray, you become a prey!

## THE WORD OF GOD

The number two obligation for every believer is the Word of God. Everything that was made was made with the Word and everything that is to be sustained is sustained by the Word. The bible said, "He sustained everything by the power of His word" - by the Word. The Word of God connects you with God because each time you read His Word you are reading what He says for all scriptures were given by the inspiration of God. At the risk of stating the obvious, one of the primary reasons to devote yourself to God's Word is because it is God's Word. The Apostle Paul states it this way: "All Scripture is God-breathed…" (2 Tim. 3:16). The Apostle Peter adds that "…no prophecy of Scripture came about by the prophet's own interpretation. For prophecy never had its origin in the will of man, but men spoke from God as they were carried along by the Holy Spirit" (2 Pet. 1:20-21). Scripture is God's Word. Therefore, each time you read and study Scripture, you are interacting with Him. He has given us a precious gift!

Many things in which we invest are temporary (for example, houses, money, possessions). The Word of the Lord, however, is eternal. Jesus declares that even though heaven and earth will pass away, His "words will never pass away" (Matt. 24:35). Peter states that "the word of the Lord stands forever" (1 Pet. 1:25). Each time you open the Word of the Lord and allow it to penetrate into your life, you are placing something eternal within you. The Word of the Lord is the Word of the Lord, it has divine power and is able to transform those who receive and accept it. The Lord makes this declaration concerning His Word: "As the rain and the snow come down from heaven, and do not return to it without watering the earth and making it bud and flourish, so that it yields seed for the sower and bread for the eater, so it is with my word that goes out from my mouth: It will not return to me empty, but will accomplish what I desire and achieve the purpose for which I sent it" (Isa. 55:10-11). The Lord's Word works powerfully and produces spiritual life.

The writer of Hebrews teaches that "the word of God is living and active. Sharper than any double-edged sword, it penetrates even to dividing soul and spirit, joints and marrow; it judges thoughts and attitudes of the heart" (Heb. 4:12). It has the power to teach, rebuke, correct, train in righteousness and equip (2 Tim. 3:16). How unfortunate it is that many Christians neglect the Lord's Word and do not give it the opportunity to deeply penetrate their lives. How wonderful, on the other hand, for those who devote themselves to God's Word. As the Psalmist states, the man who delights in God's law and meditates on it day and night are "like a tree planted by streams of water, which yields its fruit in season and whose leaf does not wither. Whatever he does prospers" (Psa. 1:2-3).

## SERVING GOD

Serving God is the third way you carry out spiritual obligation or be divinely connected to Him. He said you will serve the Lord your God Deuteronomy 28. You shall serve the Lord your God and these blessings shall come upon you. You shall serve the Lord your God and He will bless your bread and water and He would take sickness from the mist you. In Joshua 24, Joshua was saying "as for me and my house we would serve the Lord. He said choose whom you shall serve today either the God of the Amorite your father served or the True God – the living God but as for me and my house we will serve the Lord".

"Your attitude must be like my own, for I, the Messiah, did not come to be served, but to serve and to give my life." (Matt 20:28)

*We are commanded to serve God. Jesus was unmistakable: "Your attitude must be like my own, for I, the Messiah, did not come to be served, but to serve and to give my life" (Matthew 20:28 LB.).*

For Christians, service is not something to be tacked onto our schedules if we can spare the time. It is the heart of the Christian life. Jesus came "to serve" and "to give" — and those two verbs should define your life on Earth, too. Serving and giving sum up God's fourth purpose for your life.

Mother Teresa once said, "Holy living consists in doing God's work with a smile."

Jesus taught that spiritual maturity is never an end in itself. Maturity is for ministry! We grow up in order to give out. It is not enough to keep learning more and more. We must act on what we know and practice what we claim to believe. Impression without expression causes depression. Study without service leads to spiritual stagnation. The old comparison between the Sea of Galilee and the Dead Sea is still true. Galilee is a sea full of life, because it takes in water but also gives it out. In contrast, nothing lives in the Dead Sea because, with no outflow, the sea has stagnated.

The last thing many believers need is to go to another Bible study. They already know far more than they are putting into practice. What they need are serving experiences in which they can exercise their spiritual muscles.

Serving is the opposite of our natural inclination. Most of the time we're more interested in "serve us" than service. We say, "I'm looking for a church that meets my needs and blesses me," not "I'm looking for a place to serve and be a blessing." We expect others to serve us, not vice versa. But as we mature in Christ, the focus of our lives should increasingly shift to living a life of service. The mature follower of Jesus stops asking, "Who's going to meet my needs?" and starts asking, "Whose needs can I meet?"

The spiritual obligation is also carrying out God's command like what God said you should do – He said "Go ye into the world and preach the Gospel. It is a command and every Christian are designed to take this order and this is why we call it the "Great Commission". He said go ye into all the world preaching and baptizing them in the name of the father, the son and the Holy Spirit. Teaching them to observe all things that I have commanded you to do, then I am with. Remember, He said Go ye into all the nations. So, when every believer carries out this obligation, we will be guaranteed of a better future and a better generation in the world to come.

## LOVE THE WAY TO VICTORY

Our next obligation to God is Love. In Mark 11 He was speaking and He said "you shall love the Lord your God with all your heart", you cannot claim you are connected when you are not in love. My wife and I are in love but it is impossible for me to prove the love to her if am not connected with her. There must be a connection and thus the connection is a proof of love.

*"We love because he first loved us." (1 John 4:19 NIV)*

This season is a good time to remember that the reason God wants us to love is because he is love, and he created us to be like him — to love. The only reason we're able to love is because God loves us: "Love comes from God ... because God is love" (1 John 4:7-8 NIV).

We were created in God's image to do two things on Earth: Learn to love God and learn to love other people. Life is all about love. But love all started with God. He loved us first, and that gives us the ability to love others (1 John 4:19). The only reason you can love God or love anybody else is because God first loved you. And he showed that love by sending Jesus Christ to Earth to die for you. He showed that love by creating you. He showed that love by everything you have in life; it's all a gift of God's love. In order to love others and to become great lovers, we first need to understand and feel how much God loves us. We don't want to just talk about love, read about love, or discuss love; our need is to experience the love of God. We need to reach a day when we finally, fully understand how God loves us completely and unconditionally. We need to become secure in the truth that we cannot make God stop loving us.

Once we're secure inside God's unconditional love, we'll start cutting people a lot of slack. We won't be as angry as we've been. We'll be more patient. We'll be more forgiving. We'll be more merciful. We'll give others grace. But you cannot give to others what you have not received yourself, and so my hope is that, as you learn how much God loves you, you'll also let him heal your heart so that his love can flow freely through you. It's to church again, because I don't want to even see her". If you observe such people correctly, you'll realize that they are full of themselves. Never try to change anyone, the best person to change is yourself and not your wife or your spouse. When you change yourself, you'll learn to accommodate everyone and you will live in a comfortable world free of problems and woes. People are different are different and our differences in faces are also seen in our character, you can't change everybody to accommodate your presence rather being the main person to change. This would help you to avoid playing the blaming game.

In fact, you are not qualified to hate or not to talk to anybody. Somebody's weakness might be the way they talk and yours might be the way you reason everybody has a fault somewhere like I said several times in the past, the church is not a museum for saints it is a hospital for sick people. So, you can't disqualify or cast anyone down, for we all need help from above and what is from above is above all. In life, it is better not to choose your enemy to let your enemy choose you. People make statements like 'I am not talking to you again, you're not my friends. I do not want to see you again" what? This is what I called an idiotic lifestyle. We are not qualified to make that statement because Christ loves you the way you are. Christ loves you, not because you merit it, but because He just loves you.

The reason you are connected to Him is that you can love as he loves. You see why Peter asked Jesus, when he realized Jesus love people like Judas and Thomas, so Peter asked Jesus, "Master how many times would my brother, brethren offend me before I take an offence, even if I have given him seven chances?' and Jesus answered "seventy times seven" that is four hundred and ninety times in a day. There must be a kind of demon for somebody to offend you that much in a year not to talk about in one day. Sometimes, God uses fire and trails to bring out the best out of us. The way you handle people determines how God will promote you and the number of people that will follow you. Your character determines, your success with God and man. Don't that your attitude toward man and God will determine your altitude in life. Don't neglect man and then think you'll have favor with God and vice versa.

When God finds people, He found them because of their attitude. It is not all the time that you have to take the law into your own hand. Somebody insult you, just tell the person God bless you and leave the rest to God, for vengeance belongs to God. Don't let somebody else reminds you that you are born again by fighting back. Because if you fight, you are taking charge of the fight by yourself and God won't be involved and after you have fought for yourself. You are the god of yourself and you will see your temperature escalating, like boiling water in 100 degrees Celsius. Some people will even scream leave me alone like cannibals. Only animal's fights!

However, there are others who are a specialist in holding people in their heart that they are not talking to or having anything to do with them. They have various complaints regarding them. Let me explain what this really means, holding someone is your heart and complaining about them makes you not different from a madman. I madman always talk alone sometimes you will look around thinking he or she is talking to somebody but in reality, the madman is talking to the voices in his/her head. The difference between he that complained, keep grudges and the madman is that one is audible and the other is silence only to the physical eyes. In the invisible realm both, they are the same. If those grudges intensify you'll see yourself talking out loud alone and if it continues you will become mad in the real sense. so, madness is complaint and grudges to the highest degree. Now, if you're disconnected and find yourself in such situation, what is the impossible to love others until you really feel loved yourself. Take for instance a jealous husband like me I have something in me that would never allow me be at ease when I cannot hear my wife's voice or I can't to talk to her whenever I want to, the level of intimacy and love has grown to the level that I don't think I can go to days without talking to her. I am so much possessed with love for her. Each time I call without any response and the call goes into voicemail something in me begins to tremble and I become agitated simply because I am deeply in love. that's what love does in any relationship and that's how it should be with your relationship with the Maker. He loves you and wants to create an intimate relationship with you. It is written, Husbands, love your wives, just as Christ also loved the church and gave Himself up for her. His love is pure without spot and wrinkles. His love is blameless. Stay connected to him and your life will never be the same!

In that Matthew 12, Jesus was speaking further and He said that you shall love your neighbor as yourself, don't tell me you're connected with your father, the Creator of the universe when you cannot love the people He created. One of my common statements is "that none of us is better than the rest of us" – I repeat, none of us is better than the rest of us. Making yourself too high to others is in other word insulting others. People always play, the blaming game, what does that mean. It means others are always at fault nothing is wrong with you but with others. You are fast at seeing the fault of others than yourself. In such situation, it simply implies you love yourself more than you love others but God said love your neighbor as you love yourself. Not loving yourself more than your neighbors but loving them as you love yourself.

I normally hear people make a statement like this "if you see the way she looked at me, spoke to me, in fact, I am not going solution for you? Here is the solution:

*Be careful with nothing, but in everything by prayer and supplication with thanksgiving let your requests be made known unto God. And the peace of God, which passeth all understanding, shall keep your hearts and minds through Christ Jesus. Philippians 4:6-7*

*Therefore, humble yourselves under the mighty hand of God, that He may exalt you at the proper time, casting all your anxiety on Him, because He cares for you. Be of sober spirit, be on the alert. Your adversary, the devil, prowls around like a roaring lion, seeking someone to devour. (1 Peter 5:7-8)*

All in all, you have erased everybody from your life after haven prays the above verse. You cannot be connected with God particularly when you are carrying offenses. That is why God said that if you have an offense in your heart before coming to my presence, put your offering down and go and settle the problem. He said do not let the sun goes down on your discord in your heart. Simply because He loves and wants to save you from destruction.

## THE POWER OF SIN

Sin is what connects us with the affair of this world. Satan will make everything attractive to you and in fact, makes everything available to you in order to disconnect you with your Father. The values that connect you with God seem strenuous but they are not. Sin is an alternative to who you are. From the book of Genesis 3, the serpent entered Eve and asked if the woman did God say you should not eat of the fruit that is in the garden? This statement was a way to allure her into the forbidden fruits.

Sin is a deception, it is an enticement. Every sin does not start from the outside before you commit any sin, it, first of all, has to go through your mind before manifesting itself. Sin starts first as

89

a thought. The serpent went to Eve and said to her "God knows that the day you eat this fruit, you will become wise". This shows us the satanic phenomenal characteristic of enticement.

Another thing about sin does is that it makes you feel that you are wise. It makes you feel as if you are in vogue. The simplest analog for sin is those who take drugs. Maybe alcohol or weed or any other drug. When you take this drug, it controls you and makes you feel good and suddenly you start having a false identity of yourself. You stepped out, start walking and everybody else on the street seems inconsequential. Even when you don't have money in your pocket, you feel big as if you're Bill Gates. It makes you feel high and all of a sudden you become very uncontrollable and you forgot your responsibilities.

Some time ago, I was watching a comedy illustrating how rights are treated in various countries. The actor in this video was drunk and He was talking to a police officer in an abusive way. I witness an abusive drunken person being accorded respect by an American and British Police officers company meanwhile their counterpart from Nigeria was slapping the drunken man three times in the face and kicking him in the butt of the gun just to get the drunk to come to his senses.

These days people sin with impunity and they want God to comfort them in it the cops comforting the drunken man after being insulted upon. People indulge in what is wrong as if it is right. No matter what you feel about wrong, it can't make wrong right, no matter your impression. Some people come to me and say I know they have told you about me and it was me that you were talking about in your sermon and I do not care. It does not matter how you feel about sin, there is nothing you can do in your capacity to make wrong or right. Whatever is wrong is wrong and as long as you are doing it, you are wrong. Some people believe that several wrongs will correct itself and become right, that you can never be right. They're simply saying that if you owed money, several unpaid bills will pay itself. If you're in such situation, I pray that the Holy Spirit will open up your spirit to understand this is a bait from the enemy.

I was having lunch with a pastor-friend when the discussion sadly turned to a mutual friend in ministry who had failed morally. As we grieved together over this fallen comrade, now out of ministry, I wondered aloud, "I know anyone can be tempted and anyone can stumble, but he's a smart guy. How could he think he could get away with it?" Without blinking, my friend responded, "Sin makes us stupid." It was an abrupt statement intended to get my attention, and it worked.

I have often thought of that statement in the ensuing years, and I continue to affirm the wisdom of those words. How else can you explain the actions of King David, the man after God's own heart turned adulterer and murderer? Or the reckless choices of Samson? Or the public denials of Christ by Peter, the most public of Jesus' disciples? We are flawed people who are vulnerable to temptation and to the foolishness of mind that can rationalize and justify almost any course of action if we try hard enough.

If we are to have a measure of victory over the power of sin, it will come only as we lean on the strength and wisdom of Christ (Rom. 7:24-25). As His grace strengthens our hearts and minds, we can overcome our own worst inclination to make foolish choices.

The price of sin is very high Though now it may seem low; And if we let it go unchecked, its crippling power will grow. — Fitzhugh

We did say that to connect or reconnect is to join together what is separated. Therefore, when we are talking of reconnecting the disconnected generation, we are talking of rejoining man back to the values that God has installed for a man by default in the beginning. In the beginning, when God created male and female

91

and put them in the Garden, one thing He said to them is this; He said that thou may eat of everything in this garden, but of the tree of good and knowledge thou shalt not touch. He gave them instructions to follow. To reconnect with God the number one thing every person should pay attention to is the instruction of God. The bible says all scriptures are written by the inspiration of God and they are profitable to direct. Every manufacturer has a manual. Every genuine product comes with a manual. A human being is a product of God. You did not drop from the sky like the big bang theory assumed which is the highest state of foolishness and what I call intellectual nonsense. Common sense shows us that, if you looked at every creature that came from the explosion, there all look different. I looked different from my wife, other people look different from me. Next time anyone said something to you about the big bang theory just advise the person not to be stupid. Is the big bang the one that gives you breath and sustaining it? Every manufacturer that manufactured something always included in it a manual to instruct you on how to operate the item and not a big bang theory of illusion.

The manual is the wisdom guide of the manufacturer of how to successfully operate his fabricated item. Using the item without the following instruction will lead to a breakdown, chaos and short lifespan of the equipment. You have instructions as do not emerge in water, not to be operated by children etc. It is ok to have instructions because they are the connecting point that man connect to his Creator.

## WALKING IN THE POWER OF THE SPIRIT

When we are talking about disconnection, we are talking about disconnected from God. It is possible for one to disconnect by disconnecting from His instructions. Take a look into the scripture from the book of II Timothy.

*"All Scripture is God-breathed and is useful for teaching, rebuking, correcting and training in righteousness" (NIV) (II Tim 3:16)*

Let me say this to you now, anytime you go to a church where the Word of God is not being preached, all you get are motivating messages excluding sound doctrine and rebuking you as well; then consider leaving the church because you can't attain a righteous life by merely listening to a motivational speaker.

In this regard, I get disturbed sometimes when I received messages from different people taking decision of not going to church because they felt the pastor was preaches directly about them. I admonish you that should any minister preaches about you, then there must be something in you that you need to work on. However, it is a privilege for God to talk to you using the man of God. Anyway, who the Pastor should be talking about? His job is to pastor and direct you. It is called Shepherding. If the Pastor is preaching and the words of God is hitting you then the pastor has done His or her duty properly. If You cannot be corrected by the man of God, then you'll not be instructed by the "man of God". One of the reasons God gave you a minister of the gospel so that he would be able to speak into your life and destiny that which God has purposed for you.

Hosea 4:7 said, "the Lord will do nothing except He has, first of all, revealed it to His servant the Prophet". Most often, God speaks through Pastors and the Pastor did not plan what to say. He or she might simply be inspired by the Holy Spirit. So, one of the ways you will realize that you are aligned with God at any point of your life is that His word instructs, reshape, reproof, direct and rebuke you.

His words say that He will guide, the meek will He teach His ways, Surely the Sovereign LORD does nothing without revealing his plan to his servants the prophets. (KJV) (Amos 3:7)

The scriptures said the Lord will not reveal anything until the prophet is aware of it. So, you come to church and your secret has been exposed, it's a clear indication and proof that your matter has been addressed by God. There was a time I travelled to Atlanta and my host Pastor informed me that I will be teaching his worker that evening for two hours. I did not have time to prepare anything for them but the Holy Spirit gave me insight within ten minutes, I was completely given utterance, after the teaching my host said to me; "Pastor, it seemed you've been a member of our church and you know everything that was happening coupled with all we've been going through as a church. The teaching was not recorded on tape but a church worker recorded it on his personal phone so the pastor requested for it to be properly copied for others to listen to it.

After that meeting I received an invitation from Houston, I had a preaching assignment there, when I finished preaching the host pastor said he did not know that God would give me that much for them and they would have asked me to do the second service but I was already on my way to Humble Texas where I was using people as illustration in my teaching and the host pastor was crying. When I asked him why is he was crying, he said "sir, you are too much because the people you were using for illustration, we're going through the exact situation in which you were talking about. He said not only did you gave perfect examples the words were also appropriate for the illustration but you also used the right people for the illustrations. That was why he placed his hands on his head crying heavily. I never had an idea of what the church was going through as at then but through the help of holy spirit I was able to minister the divine and ordained message needed at that particular time. All this happened because I was walking in the power of the spirit.

God reveals secrets in the heart of His servant in order to reconnect his people to Himself. If you stop hearing what would rebuke, instruct, correct and discipline you, then you know that you are losing the love of God. The bible says that he that the father loved, him he chastised. Let me say a good thing about this, it is not only the chastisement He sends, He sends you the Word of grace, the word of hope, the word of promotion, the word of faith and the word of healing.

The kingdom of darkness deceives most Christians to choose or pick only what we suit them, such as I want the Word of healing so I pick that one and leave the rest, or I want a word on prosperity and we discard the rest. The word of correction – oh no not me why correction I have not done anything wrong so we just choose what we want. I want to only hear nice things about myself. If you are a Christian that selects or picks only what you want then you become a spoilt child of God. Children that are so picky ended up becoming spoiled. Don't pick or choose, received the entire and engrafted word of God. The bible said we are no longer children who will be fed with the milk of the word of God but strong meat. Strong meat will reconnect you with the father. Criticism, rebuke or correction from God are there to refine you and make you into a better person.

"Criticism may not be agreeable, but it is necessary. It fulfills the same function as pain in the human body. It calls attention to an unhealthy state of things." —Winston Churchill

Critics only make you stronger. You have to look at what they are saying as feedback. Sometimes the feedback helps, and other times, it's just noise that can be a distraction. —Robert Kiyosaki

# CHAPTER 10

# STAY FOCUS AND AVOID DISTRACTION

---

Distractions as a whole are a huge drain on every aspect of who we are. It takes our focus away from what we should be doing - our tasks, goals and purpose. This is why we have to eliminate them from our lives if possible! Distraction is one of the greatest weapons against our generation Distraction is anything and everything that we occupy our time and hindered us from achieving our purpose. You might be seated right now and reading this book, and the devil is there trying to take your mind off what you are reading by simply causing your mind and thought to move to and FRO like a roaring lion.

A restaurant owner in the village of Abu Ghosh, just outside Jerusalem, offered a 50-percent discount for patrons who turned off their cell phones. Jawdat Ibrahim believes that smartphones have shifted the focus of meals from companionship and conversation to surfing, texting, and business calls. "Technology is very good," Ibrahim says. "But . . . when you are with your family and your friends, you can just wait for half an hour and enjoy the food and enjoy the company." How easily we can be distracted by many things, whether in our relationship with others or with the Lord.

Jesus told His followers that spiritual distraction begins with hearts that have grown dull, ears that are hard of hearing, and eyes that are closed (Matt. 13:15). Using the illustration of a farmer scattering seed, Jesus compared the seed that fell among thorns to a person who hears God's Word but whose heart is focused on other things. "The cares of this world and the deceitfulness of riches choke the word, and he becomes unfruitful". There is great value in having times throughout each day when we turn off the distractions of mind and heart and focus on the Lord.

O Lord, help me to turn off all the distractions around me and focus on You. May my heart be good soil for the seed of Your Word today.

"If you are always on the go and you can't hear God, you are facing the barrier of busyness."

Distraction is a thing that satisfies our feeling but it might be taking your mind off from another important thing. Distraction is like moving around us when something important is going on. It defocus us from whatever we are focusing on initially. So, you woke up to have a shower but a call came in suddenly and distracted you while on your way to the bathroom. As you were on the way to the bathroom when the call came in, you attended to the call, immediately the call was over, something else caught your attention you attended to that as well and rather than going straight to the bathroom you attended to something else in the meantime perambulating around the house but still want to have a shower, until your entire initial programme changed.

However, what is a distraction? Distraction is anything that derails you from your God-given purpose. When God gives you a gift, you have to hold tightly and firmly so that the enemy won't take it from you. I learned a little lesson when I was growing up as a kid, all my siblings were trained in such a way that you had to focus all your attention on the task at hand rather than splitting your attention into several tasks. We're five of us and as kids, we always eat in the same bowl. Sometimes we will use tricks to derail the other person attention, just to get a bigger share of the person' food. The older ones often harbor the ambition to distract the others like to get me water or bring a knife and so much tricks, when indeed none of those things were necessary. So, while the person who is fetching the water or the knife is out, a piece of meat would have disappeared and as soon as that happened the others will become wise and each person would hold their meat in the hand.

You can't hear God when your mind is crowded with thoughts, worries, fears, and plans, or if you always have the radio or TV on. And if you constantly have your phone against your ear, when God calls all he gets is a busy signal! All of these distractions are what Jesus was referring to in Luke 8 when he talked about the seed falling in the weeds. Today's verse says those weeds grew with the seed and strangled it. Now notice that this scenario is a little bit better than the shallow soil because the seed actually sprouts and grows. But the weeds choke it out so it never bears fruit. So many people hear God speak, but as they go on their way, life's worries, riches, and pleasures choke them, so they never mature.

Often, we confuse busyness with productivity and they aren't the same thing. If you keep going, going, going but you aren't spiritually growing, growing, growing, you are busy, not productive. Jesus says distractions are like weeds that grow up in your mind and heart, just as weeds grow in a garden.

There are three types of weeds that will keep you from hearing God's voice:

**1. Worries:** The Greek word for worry is merinma, which means "pulled in different directions." When you are pulled in different directions, you are worried. And when you are worried, you can't hear God.

**2. Riches:** You can be so busy making a living, trying to make money to pay the bills and get out of debt that you can't hear God.

**3. Pleasures:** God gives you pleasures, and they are a good thing. But you can get so busy pursuing pleasures and fun that you forget to pursue God as well.

How much effort does it take to grow weeds? None. Weeds are a sign of neglect. When you neglect your time with God, the weeds start to grow in your life. In order to overcome the weeds, you must learn to overcome your preoccupied mind.

First Kings 19:12 says that when God spoke to Elijah, it wasn't in a wind or earthquake or fire; it was in a gentle whisper. If you want to hear God whisper to you, you have to be quiet.

Also In the parable of the talent, the bible says the master gave one five talents, another two talents, and another one. The talent was not distributed or shared equally but one thing is certain we all have 24 hours a day and equal opportunity to succeed. No matter how small your talent is, it has the possibility of expansion except that you want to bury it. You go to work and earned six pounds and fifty pence per hour and someone else goes to work and earned sixty-five pounds per hour and another person goes to work and earned six hundred and fifty pounds per hour, the difference here is what those people have done before with their hours. Some have gone to college to study medicine, have grafted hard, study day and night, now working earning that sum of money. Therefore, use your time well and invest it in the appropriate task and calling. You need to remember that while one was studying hard, the others were playing, facebooking, playing with all sort of things. At the starting point, everybody has equal time, everybody has an equal life but one was distracted thus became a failure.

Distraction in our life is to truly stop us from what we should really become. Most people will die less than they ought to be. Dr. Myles Munroe once said that "the richest place on the face of the earth is the graveyard". Let me ask you this, are you truly the best you can be or how can you truly rate yourself in terms of being successful? Is this the best pastor you can be, is this the best we can be as a church? Stop watching everything around you happening rather be the pioneer of new things happening. In life there are actors and there are spectators. The best person you should strive to be is to be an actor rather than fans or a spectator of the things happening.

Many of us allow things to happen by default, we expect success to happen by default without realizing that every minute you spend wrongly is a wrong investment. Just like Stock trading, you understand that in Stock trading you can get a market right or wrong by making a wrong decision in one second. If you have been watching the stock traders, you will notice that they can have up to six screens going in front of them at any one time and the person in front of the screen is determined and not distracted by anything else going around him or her. He or she is just watching the screen to determine the best time to enter or exit a position. By entering or existing at the right time the person will be laughing always at the bank.

Like the stock trader, you have to be focused and determined. The act of focus is to connect you to your ultimate goal from God meanwhile distraction is to defocus you. We know what the Word of God says that we should pray, read the Word, etc.; but the devil will bring so many distractions within our 24 hours that we would not be able to spend even five minutes in the word of God. You should be evangelizing and inviting people to Christ but you spend seven days a week all about you but none about God. Some people are so dry spiritually and too dry to the extent that they have even given up praying. Some have lost every zest of spirituality that the only connection with God is when they are in church. Some no longer have no attention for the Word of God, no desire for prayer and now they cannot even pray for five minutes until they have accepted it as the norm. It has become their now normal lifestyle not to pray. The devil has distracted them and taken them astral. However, we thank God for His grace because He said His grace is sufficient and can take us off every situation. His grace can put us back on track.

With today's modern world, the Internet is just so available that instead of someone picking up a book and read, there are other things to look or read about on the internet. Recently, I took a stock and look at myself and the time with those who have pastored me in the past and some of them I called my fathers were pastoring their church when there were any mobile phones, no internet etc. They had more time to study the Word of God than watching the media which in most cases is man and Satan's means to control the world. These days people get offended that I have not called them or responded to their text or email. If I was responding to call my calls as there come, by now I would have been a garbage can. In this life, two things are certain, either people control your life or you take control of life by yourself. It is either you let your precious time to be managed by yourself or people will help you manage it for you and managing it of cause for their own need and pleasure. Those who are close to me can testify of the number of calls that come to my phone on daily basis. I can't accept them, I am not a sales manager or except you do not want me to fulfill my assignment or purpose that I will be answering everything. No matter how much I love you, I cannot respond to everything. Sometimes I finished on the phone with one person or another then I'll realize that I have spent 45 minutes to one hour on the phone with just one person. For me to have five or ten of such conversations in a day, that would-be radio stations and tell me how I am supposed to get on with my assignment or purpose? Out of the twenty-four hours you have in a day, you have to sleep for eight hours, that is one-third of your day already done, you have also spent another eight hours on the internet and social media. Now tell me how many hours is remaining to connect with God or to connect with your destiny? So, if you have to go to school, prepare to study, prepare to connect to God.

## THE BENEFIT OF BOOKS

I have come across people who will be walking with a small book of about 120 pages for about two months and are unable to finish it, simply because of lack of focus. In fact, some have not been able to read up to 4 or 5 books a year but they can tell which movie is out and the head style of a certain celebrity. Is it that the book that hard or is it because they are distracted? Books are necessary and very essential. Books carry the secret of the wise or put it this way the wisdom of others. Reading books can be interpreted as tapping and absorbing from the wisdom of others, the wisdom tapped will help you stand far above trials and defeats. For example, if you want to start a business, you can conclude that you know it all, of course, you know something about it but you-you read a book that business you simply taking other people's wisdom and adding it on your own for a giant leap in business. Readers are leaders in business or ministry, therefore my friend read books until you discover yourself through the book you're reading. If you are reading and someone else wants your attention and you closed the book with a good intention to come back to it in another thirty minutes. You can forget it because you might not come back to that book for another three days to four days, this is what distraction does to you.

Let us see what the bible says about distraction as we look at the book of Corinthians again. I refused to be distracted:

*"I am saying this for your own good, not to restrict you, but that you may live in a right way in undivided devotion to the Lord." (Corinthians 7:35)*

Radio, Internet, News, Celebrity gossip, social medias that we all like to catch up with might be there to distract us. A phone call may be important but may not be the right time, every important thing has its own time. Doing the right thing at the wrong is the distraction. Not every important thing will necessarily be a priority for your own life.

For instance, let assume my friend committed an offence and the police intervened. He is asking me to come and help him sort out his mistake while I am working on my own assignment. At this, his priority is not my priority but he might take the view that I have abandoned him at his time of need but it is not so. His priority is not my priority and he will need to sort out his own mess or his stupidity and allow me to focus on what I am doing. For I will only come to his rescue only when I am done with my assignment, by so doing he would have learnt from his stupidity.

Don't let other people stupidity put your life and in catastrophic jeopardy. Live life the way God has created it, and enjoy the best of it by doing the assignment that he created you for; only then would you be able to enjoy the best of life. I am a man of purpose and born for a reason, nothing will stop me to fulfill my mission and task on earth. Sometimes, I tell my church members to have all their papers or car document up to date so that we can save time and not get into mess or bother anyone with issues which may not be necessary. You can save a lot of time and errors of your stupidity by doing things right in the first place. The man that knows where he is going will always do the right thing.

we might talk on the phone for two minutes but if you are keeping me on the phone for up to ten minutes please understand that you are eating into my destiny. Every conversation you are having should be programmed and timed. When you attend to work and you are paid six pounds and fifty pence an hour, that one-hour conversation you just had is worth six pounds fifty to you? I know how much I am a worth an hour and at this current time of my life, I should be paid more than money can value because my time is my life and you can't pay for it. So, understand that when I am talking to somebody for more than ten minutes it should be someone that I am mentoring, training, instructing or coaching and when our conversation does not fall into those categories understand that we need to be brief, concise and finish the conversation in time.

Don't let other people put their weight and burden on you by eating up your time. Take your life seriously and do the same with your conversations. A fruitless conversation should be cut off. If it profiteth you nothing cut it short and don't allow distraction to eat into your destiny. Don't let friends and relatives distract you, remember that those who make news don't watch the news and everything we have the players and spectators, be the players. Players train and they are very conscious of their time. Take your life more serious, take your family more serious, take your children more serious, take your spouse more serious, take your God much more serious. If you have institutions around your life, give them priority, give them the attention they deserve. You cannot be talking about your business and allow other things to distract you. Give your business your utmost attention.

Look at yourself and boldly proclaim 'I am divinely connected''. As soon as you say, you will find yourself energy with the spirit of boldness. You will be equipped energy to clear off every distraction. Say it with faith in your heart that I am divinely connected and Lord I want more of you, Lord I desire more of you". When we asked for more of God, we are asking for more of his grace and praying that Holy Spirit will help us to be more aligned with God's will for our life.

## PREACHING AND TEACHING

As we conclude this book of reconnecting the disconnected generation I want you to understand that there is the difference between teaching and preaching. I want you to understand this distinction so that you can be connected with the vision God has given unto you and to be connected to the giver of this vision. When you give your life to Christ or when you become born again, you need to be taught the word, so you require teaching. You need teaching,

In Matthew 28 Jesus said to the disciples "go ye into all the world and preach the gospel" that is the good news.

The difference between preaching and teaching is preaching is kind of motivating while teaching is informing and dissecting the word for easy digestion and absorption. Preaching kind of give you the goose boom of excitement without breaking the word into nutritional manner for you to digest. As a believer, you still need preaching because you still require some motivation but the Word of God is what we preach as pastors. However, if the pastor is not preaching the Word of God, he or she is just a motivational speaker, comedians or a storyteller. But when you hear a teacher speaking, and when you attend their seminars, you can't hold it but take notes. They deliver the Word with such clarity and funfair that you are clear about which direction to go.

For example, talk on how to start a business and how to start anything though a motivational speaker can do it nevertheless, the teacher will digest it to you with a clear spiritual understanding which at the same time is able to discern your need at that point in time. So when we go to the church what we hear is more than motivational talks.

"Unbelievers are to be preached to, believers are to be taught."

Jesus commanded the disciples to go into the world and preach to all nations baptizing them and to teach them to observe all things

*Therefore, go and make disciples of all nations, baptizing them in the name of the Father and of the Son and of the Holy Spirit, and teaching them to obey everything I have commanded you. And surely, I am with you always, to the very end of the age." (NIV) (Matthew 28:19)*

Observe the stages of development Jesus instructed which they had to go through, As an unbeliever they are to be preached to when they become believers they are to be baptized and to be taught. The purpose of the teaching is for them to observe and do because it is by observing and doing that they will be able to be sustained by the word of God, in moment trails and temptations.

The Holy Spirit always reminds me that my assignment is not to preach to the body Christ but to teach. During teaching, some received the milk of the word, other strong meat and some wine dimension of the word, depending on the direction the Holy Spirit is a ministry to the people. Sometimes during preaching those spiritual babes who are low in spirit will be motivated by what is been preached, those who need correction will be corrected, those who require strong meat will be fed and healing will take place, and people will be saved, hallelujah.

Scriptures say, "teaching them to observe all things that have been instructed". so, teachers will bring to the church whatever has been commended and instructed. Instructed here means they have been taught as well that is why they are required to teach. Teaching moves us closer to the coming of our Lord Jesus Christ.

There are things God is speaking on the inside that He brings out at the appropriate time, but only at the appropriate time. He said whatever I have commanded you, so I am with you even to the end of the world. Teaching can never mislead rather it direct, the divine inspired teaching of the cause. Teaching move us closer in readiness for the coming of our Lord Jesus Christ and the coming may be in the form of rapture or we die and go to heaven.

You don't go to church or Christian fellowship because it is spiritually right but rather because it is connected with instruction. You've got to be connected with direction. If you are in a church for two hours, you heard the Word and you remain the same then something must know something is wrong, you have to drive and thirst for more of God and desire to know Him more in his presence.

As teachers, pastors and ministers of the Gospel, we have to live by the Word. The word has to be our status quo for ministry and life. We have to teach the body of Christ the Word. Teachings bring kingdom expansion. Don't let hypocrisy intervene in your ministry, curse it off your life and ministry. Jesus was not afraid to call the Pharisees and the Sadducee's hypocrite because they taught people to observe the law and yet did not practice what they taught. You are a hypocrite if you go to church but your life does not reflect that of Christ. No matter your situation, if you're struggling with any situation of life or sin, His mercy is there to rescue and deliver you, right now whereas you're reading this book. Jesus simply calls Him from the depth of your heart and tell him Lord help me and receive the grace you have made available and insufficiency for me. That simple prayer can turn your whole life around for good.

Some believers have gotten too used to living in the world as if the world is our final destination. Some are so ungodly that ungodliness seems fine as a normal way of life. As earlier said, one of the reasons why God gave us Pastors, is that the Pastor might speak into our life. Pastors are a shepherd and when you look at the scenery of the shepherd and the flock, you'll see that the shepherd has many flocks and he is always trying to guide them and to keep them on the track. If you have been living a wayward life and have not been spiritually connected to your Source, the Creator, I am calling you today to get back into the camp in Jesus' name.

Some people are different on every day of the week. They have seven characters for the week; Christian or saint on Sunday, club member on Friday, a worker on Monday, Tuesday Gossipers, on Wednesday backsliders, and so on. The only way you'll see such people Holy and be Christian like is only on Sunday. In fact, they automatically put on the Christian coat of conduct on Sunday and as soon as they leave the church, everything about God vamps from their spirit. This kind of life is a mess and disgraceful to the Christendom. It is better to be either an unbeliever or a believer than being a mixture of sand and sugar. Living such a life is a tremendous frustration and it often happens like this when such believers don't know who Christ is. They have mistaken Christianity to religion or religious activities.

## REMEMBER THE SON OF WHOM YOU ARE

"Stay connected to the tree of life. Stay connected to the way that is right Stay connected to the creative power Christ is the tree of life stay connected"

Do you call yourself a Christian? If so you need to remember who you are. Yes, we are sons and daughters of God, we are also slaves with a to God. As a result, we have a new master we have a responsibility to live and serve him. If our life doesn't match up to the position we profess, you need to ask yourself "do I belong to god at all?" Believers are called not called only to talk

109

the talk, but actually walk the walk." Evidence of a true believer is not only found in our words, the ordinances we partake in, the bible we truths we uphold - but in the very outworking of our daily lives.... Being a Christian is more than some decision you made one night (many people are being duped today that they are Christians) yet their lives simply contradict it!

Matt 7:21 Jesus said, not everyone who says to me lord, lord, will enter the kingdom of heaven, but only he who does the will of my father who is in heaven. So, let's remember who we are...

In John 15, He says I am the vine and you are the branches, you cannot have branches that are not connected to it will wither away. The reason why some people are dry is that they are out of His presence. There is no branch that can live outside of its source when you are disconnected from your source you are ever resourceful. You cannot be called by the name of Christ and not be connected to him. The connection is a choice, you've to boldly and willingly make the choice to stay connected to God the master, for He is your source. Your life is primarily and principally His, every time and anytime you engage in other activities you are burrowing yourself into those activities.

When we were growing up and we have to go and stay with a friend or relative, the word of our parents "remember the son of whom you are" always rings in our spirit. If you have to travel abroad, it is the same message for those of us that come from the western part of Nigeria the message is the same "remember the child of whom you are." Some few years back, the President of Nigeria was going to award a contract to a family we know, it was a big contract to build a local airport, I was privileged to go and visit the construction while it was on-going. On my way, I read in the national newspaper that before the contract was awarded, the President asked for the father of the chief contractor to meet with him. When the chief contractor's father met with the president the discussion was that he reminded his son the chief contractor whose child he's. The president said the father should remind the chief contractor that the job that is to be done is for the country. So, it has to be done well to protect the name and reputation of the family and on the other hand if the project was badly executed and embezzlement took place the chief contractor will be bringing shame on the country and his family.

So, in the same way as a child of God, we ought to protect the name of God and the kingdom of which we belong. We are born of God and we came from a royal family, whatever we do we do it in the name of that family as ambassadors. That's one of the reasons why when you hear a Christian or pastor does something wrong, people always amplify it and conclude that all Christians are alike, simply because one person or some people corrupted the name of our Father with their character and dubious act. Every act, every behavior, everything that we do is either bringing glory or shame or disrepute to the name of Christ. Therefore, I encourage you, as a chosen generation to protect your kingdom royalty.

You know, we said one of the ways people get disconnected is through sin and the second one is a distraction. Sin, for example, connects you to the wrong source meanwhile distraction takes you off track. However, how does sin connect one to other negative sources? Let assume, someone commit fornication or adultery. You know before the process, such a person thought about it and mind was always thinking about the person in which he had to commit the sin with, even when the sin is committed the same is joint to that harlot and is one with her. Even after he leaves the harlot, you will always find him going back there, simply because there is an established connection in the bloodline that needs to be disconnected by the person can be free completely by grace. Distraction, on the other hand, is what the scripture calls weight in the book of Hebrews; it asks us to lay aside every weight and sin that every get us astray. You now see that these two major factors are the enemy of progress. There are the things can always disconnect one from his source. I decree that as you are reading this book, your life will never remain the same, you'll receive grace to overcome in Jesus' name. I pray today that you will overcome distraction completely in the name of Jesus.

## FOLLOW THE LEADING OF THE SPIRIT

I read a book written by brother Sai, a great man of God who God used tremendously to establish churches in India and the rest of Asia. He died at a very good old age in his 80s. He started following Jesus as early as when he was 18 years old. Brother Sai started service at ten o'clock in the morning and started preaching at about one O'clock in the afternoon until about seven pm at night and people were still sitting there listening to his teaching. He did this for over forty years and when some people were complaining that the service was too long, the Holy Spirit will ask him to ask the person murmuring or complaining why such a person was still there, he reminded them that was what God has called him to do. As he did this person was getting healed, getting blessed and prosperity was increasing. We cannot be selective Christians who pick and choose what we want to hear and what we do not want.

All Scripture is God-breathed and is useful for teaching, rebuking, correcting and training in righteousness. (2 Timothy 3:16) We have to take the word as it comes to us. Selective Christian pick and choose which precept of God to act upon and what to disregard. If you are a Christian you have to be holistic as a Christian and everything He has to say you have to be connected with.

For example, in my ministry, I have 7 pillars that the Lord has directed me to establish my ministry on. Sometimes He laid in my heart which one I am to share with the people of God. In such situation, I always feel His Spirit pushing me to share that one particular topic to His people. Let say, He wants me to teach on values, Christ, Hope, and Glory and He is speaking to me expressly that I have to teach on these four values because it has a lot to do with shaping and sustaining His people. In this situation, I can't resist and minister only what my flesh feels or minister only what the people want which in most cases is fleshly control. Refusing to minister according to His divine leading will be bringing the church into damnation. I wish to encourage reading this book, to always follow the leading of the Holy Spirit because He is the builder of churches and lives. He said to Peter through Jesus Christ, that upon you Peter, I will build my church and the gate of hell shall not prevail. He was simply telling Peter that he will build a sustaining ministry through peter and hell which troubles, sickness, disasters, confusion, shall not come over it.

No matter what the teaching I am teaching in my church, I always have to make sure it is related and connected to the key pillars of the ministry. I can't go off topic simply because I am not the one building the church but Christ. He is the master that draws and write the spiritual curriculum of my ministry. He is the author and finisher of my faith and ministry. I do this because it enables me to stay connected to the Creator, the one who sits on the throne and send us with this mandate of glory.

I often ask myself why is it that some religion becomes more radicalized to the point where they are willing to die. The answer is they have been taught. They have been taught something that convinces them right deep into their spiritual DNA and up to point where their own life becomes worthless. For example, the Islamic Sect the Al Qaeda, when they want to destroy a city or building, they became solely consumed by the idea that they are doing it for God and as a result, they can even care about their lives. Only mercy can serve such people from committing suicides in the name of God. The teaching they have received, have a stronger purpose in them than their own life. Their life is not worth much unless they fight for something that is bigger than their life. They have been painted a picture that is bigger than their life, they have been sold something that says their life is not worthy unless they do something which tangible to their eyes.

When we as ministers of the Gospel teach the ministry to visualize nothing else but the glory this will give them the power and energy to see beyond the obstacle. This will also give them the ability to right beyond all odds. The picture my ministry connects through as a church is the picture of Glory that is Christ in us is the hope of Glory. In other words, we are connecting through the Word to let people know that their tomorrow is better than their today in all aspects of their life. God gave us this guarantee because "He said beloved I which above all things that you may prosper and be in health even as your soul prospereth". So, His number one wishes above all things are prosperity. His wishes are His will which is from above and whatever is from above is above all. God wants you to be always above and to be the head and not the tail because he has called you and chosen you as a chosen generation. You are a royal people and very peculiar.

## NOW IS THE TIME

Now is the time for you to apprehend this word right deep into your spirit. It is in your apprehension that you will fully enjoy the benefit of his Word. It is the time for you to be free and connected to Him. Now is the time; John the Baptist called the unfaithful generation. "generations of a viper". Such generation was a disconnected generation. However, if you have been disconnected in any way now is the time for you to reconnect to Him. Don't wait until it becomes too late. God's kingdom operates with time and if you have to work with God you have to understand that there is time for everything. If you have to reconnect with God you have to understand that you have to use your time meaningfully. When you missed out on the time to reach God it becomes more and more difficult for you to reach Him. This was why King David said "early will I seek you, three times I will pray and seven times will I dance in your presence". No matter how busy King David was, ten times he has time for God in a day.

According to Ecclesiastes 3:1-8, wisdom recognizes that everything in life has its own season—in human activities as in the realm of nature. "There is a season, a time for every purpose under heaven" (3:1). Perhaps you are getting married or becoming a parent for the first time. Maybe you are leaving school and entering the workforce, or moving from fulltime work to retirement. As we move from season to season, our priorities change. We may need to put aside what we did in the past and funnel our energy into something else. When life brings changes in our circumstances and obligations, we must responsibly and wisely discern what kind of commitments we should make, seeking in whatever we do to "do all to the glory of God" (1 Cor. 10:31). Proverbs 3:6 promises that as we acknowledge Him in all our ways, He will guide us in the way we should go.

Daniel was a President and when he was instructed to stop praying, he did not only refuse to stop praying but Daniel increased the number of times he prayed and he opened his window for the whole city to see him do it. If you want to connect with God, you must set a regular time to study and to have with God. God must be embedded into your time, every day of your life you must have space set apart for God. Like Daniel, when we wake up in the morning, the first thing we have to say is Good morning God, good morning Jesus and good morning Holy Spirit then you turn to your spouse and even a child that is unborn in me will know how to say that, and you say good morning dad and good morning mother. This is for you to have an understanding that you have a heavenly father and you recognize that. Even if due to any reason you woke up late and you have thirty minutes left to set off for work, at least three minutes of that should be set aside for God which shows that you still reference God, for you to have enough time to say "Hallelujah father I woke up late but I just want to give you thanks and return all the glory back to you because I know you will give me the strength to wake up two hours earlier tomorrow and I know that you will help me to be more organized I love you lord thanks for hearing me." Then you must ensure that you find time to read His word, listen to audio sermons and you set time apart to be with Him always. God deserves personal relationship with you. God created you for his mandate not for yourself and for everyone is ready to live according to his lay down precept should have the understanding that Satan the source of distraction wants to break that connection.

Satan is the source of all forms of disconnection believers experience in this generation, and if he knows you are thirsty for God, he will throw all sort of challenges your way to distract you from that walk of faith. "I prophesy into your life as you are reading this book that your life will go from strength to strength and from glory to glory in the name of Jesus. The higher you want to go in your walk with God the greater the distraction you will face. The deeper you want to grow with God the higher the temptation and trials. I normally say "a new level, a new devil". The higher you want to fly with God, the higher will be your challengers. The engine required for Ferrari or Lamborghini is different from the engine required for a family pleasure car, but if the car must fly it requires the engine of an aircraft, otherwise it will not fly. We have many Christians today even though they have given their lives to Jesus many years ago, yet crawling. They cannot run alone not to talk of flying. Note that it is the size of your engine that determines the height of your flight and the engine must be fortified, tried and tested. This is the reason why you are going through temptation, challenges, and trials. Things might be getting tougher, more challenging and more difficult, don't worry because it is a preparation for greater things. The testing of your faith worketh patience.

Have that burning desire in you to soar like an eagle for that who Christ like you to. Don't try to fly like a parrot for you'll get eaten up by the way and people will be tired of your too much speaking without strength. The Holy Spirit once said to me "As you begin to run, get ready to fly because very soon as you run so fast, you will begin to fly. You will get to the point where it will become so scary and much difficult but if you can just maintain that momentum then you begin to fly high and higher. Once you start flying, you have much more speed, make less noise and it becomes scarier that you won't be able to understand with your human sense".

*So that the man of God may be complete and proficient, well fitted and thoroughly equipped for every good work.". (1 Timothy 3:17)*

# CHAPTER 11

# GET CONNECTED TO GOD

B ut Jesus looked at them and said, *"With man this is impossible, but with God all things are possible." Matthew 19:26*

As we move through our busy, hectic lives on a synchronized mission of daily events plotted out in bold headlines on our calendars and "to do" lists, we realize the importance we have placed on functioning technology to pull us along and keep us gripped to our everyday schedules, while allowing us to efficiently manipulate and accomplish many tasks in our daily lives.

Our cell phones and computers require charging and plugging into a power source. We need cell towers, data plans, Internet providers, power surge protectors, fire walls, and secure passwords - and that's just to be able to be linked to everyone and everything immediately. It's all for the purpose of making the busy even busier by allowing us to cram more into our 86,400 seconds we have in a day. Have you ever thought about how much trust and reliance we place in these devices to run our lives?

*"I am the vine; you are the branches. If you remain in me and I in you, you will bear much fruit; apart from me you can do nothing." John 15:5*

119

This Bible verse arrests me in my thinking and gives me great reason to rethink everything. What if we stay plugged in and connected to our Creator with the same unmatched enthusiasm? What if we were to give God the same dedication, reliance and trust that we give to our small plugged in know-it-alls? Would we not have the most amazing life if we started our days supercharged in the Lord and completely connected to the ultimate of all power sources? The connection that is always reliable, the one that is never subject to error, the one that can't break down or become obsolete. The one source that can never be hacked, breeched, or compromised! The highly functional, trustworthy, super intelligent, miraculous, omniscient kind of connection that can conclusively never fail!

## WAYS OF GETTING CONNECTED WITH GOD

We get connected to God through Prayer – Isaiah 1:18-19.

It's time to talk directly to God. Instead of relying on anyone else to tell you what God wants for your life, start a direct conversation with Him. Tell Him what is on your mind. Tell Him your concerns. Ask for what you need and even what you want. Pray for the needs of others. And, believe that what you ask will be answered.

*"Come now, and let us reason together, says the Lord. Though your sins are like scarlet, they shall be as white as snow; though they are red like crimson, they shall be like wool. If you are willing and obedient, you shall eat the good of the land;" (Isaiah 1:18-19)*

Prayer is a communication channel between you and the creator. The relationship that you have with your spouse intensify as you stay connected with her/him in communication. Any relationship whereby there is lack of communication is liable to collapse. WHY? Because communication is the bedrock for intimacy. Everybody wants communication, even the dog in your house communication; whenever you isolate your dog or cat any pet, it feels frustrating. Therefore, if animals and humans cherish communication then what about God?

Prayer affords you the opportunity to communicate with God. We need to Understanding that we must grow our prayer capacity, and to communicate on regular basis with God. Five minutes here and ten minutes there, and so on and so forth, then you shall soon get the grasp of it. So, if you have not been praying on a regular basis I am urging you to start now. Look for prayer meetings and groups that can enable you to catch the fire of prayer. The human spirit in most cases, find it difficult to pray and to meditate on the Word. Sometimes we lost the zeal and in such situation, the best way to gain it is by praying with others.

Make prayer a lifestyle. Pray with your family members, etc. Make it a habit to always be praying together with your family before you leave home in the morning and if you live alone to pray and charge up your spirit before you leave. Even while you are in the bathroom, you should still be able to speak to your heavenly father. Start by saying "good morning God, good morning Lord Jesus and good morning Holy Spirit you can then continue your conversation with your heavenly father with reference to Him.

Let me say this to you, the devil does not want this to happen, so he will seize the opportunity to remind you of why your prayers will not be answered or by reminding you that you have sinned. Do not by this lies relent your effort to pray, this is the Devil's job and the reason why he is called the accuser of brethren. Remember that whilst we were yet sinners and far away from God, our heavenly father had forgiven all your sins and demonstrated His love for you and His only son died for you.

*"But God demonstrates His own love toward us, in that while we were still sinners, Christ died for us." (Romans 5:8 NKJV)*

Always thinking about sin is a devilish act to help condemn

you, the scripture says "they are therefore now no condemnation to those who are in Christ Jesus". Your sin has been forgotten don't let the devil hold you captive with it, by deceitfully helping you to proclaim your sins in the name of the prayer of confession. Your confession should be done immediately after the act is committed or omitted, not when you wake up to pray. The bible says in the book of Romans 3:23 that there is none of us without sin.

*"for all have sinned and fall short of the glory of God," (Romans 3:23)*

It was further buttressed in Romans 5:5, that while we are sinners, God demonstrated his love for us by allowing His only son to die for.

*"But God demonstrates his own love for us in this: While we were still sinners, Christ died for us." (Romans 5:8)*

In your sin Christ knows you, so follow his procedures, you hallow His name and begin to pray for things to happen. Pray for growth in the church, the nation, pray for His kingdom to be established, pray for your pastor to have utterances, pray for the prime minister and other people in government including your local authority to rule well.

There is a presidential election and you do not know which side or who to vote for, pray Lord let "thy will be done". You have two suitors, one is rich and the other one is "rich" too, one is dark and the other one is a fair cry out to the father, "Lord thy will be done concerning this situation in my life". Then you start praying for yourself and your needs, "Lord give me my daily bread". God is willing to answer your prayers in all circumstance. He wants you to be called blessed. Fruitfulness is the first commandment God gave to man. He said "be fruitful and multiply.

## AND OUR DAILY BREAD!

As Jesus continued to teach us about prayers, He said we

should ask the father for our daily bread. Therefore, it is certain that they must be daily supply from the father above. Before you do so, you have to ask for forgiveness of sin by forgiving others. You will have to pray like this "Father please forgive my trespasses, please cleanse me of all my unrighteousness. I want to be strong but I found myself being a weak, yesterday I asked you for forgiveness about this sin, I did it again Lord please forgive me and help me not to fall into the trap of this sin again." Now you also have to forgive other people who have offended you, you cannot hold other people in your heart and be asking for forgiveness. Your heart needs to be liberated from all unforgiveness. You have to release all that you are holding in your heart, once you have released others, you'll begin to enjoy an open flow of peace and open heaven over your life. Also, you have to believe in your heart that you have been forgiven.

## THE WORD OF GOD.

In Psalm 23, David said, the Lord is my shepherd; He makes me lie down in the green pasture. The word of God is the Pasture that is green. The word of God is the pathway and the light that direct every destiny. The word has to be in your mouth and mind daily because it will give you an ultimate direction for your life and destiny. The word will make you overcomers. The word of God is powerful for so many reasons.

First, the Word of God is infallible. There is no error in God's Word. The law of the Lord is perfect concerning our soul. The testimony of the Lord is not only infallible it is inerrant. Proverbs 30:5-6, "Every word of God is pure; He is a shield to those who put their trust in Him. Do not add to His words, Lest He rebuke you, and you be found a liar." The purity of His words does not need anything added to it. God warns us not to misrepresent His scripture.

Second, the Word of God is complete. The Bible does not need any new chapters or verses. It is all given to us already. Many cults add their own books or commentaries to the Bible. All you need is God's Word because it is the holy Word of God. It is complete. In Revelation 22:18-19, God gives us a warning, "For I testify to everyone who hears the words of the prophecy of this book: If anyone adds to these things, God will add to him the plagues that are written in this book; and if anyone takes away from the words of the book of this prophecy, God shall take away his part from the Book of Life, from the holy city, and from the things which are written in this book."

Third, the Word of God is totally authoritative. The book of Psalms 119:89 says, "Forever, O LORD, your word is settled in heaven." The Word of God is the only source for absolute divine authority. This divine authority is for you and me as servants of Jesus Christ. When some say, "I have a word from the Lord for you," write it down and as you study God's word see if the Lord speaks to you through His Scriptures. Only then will you know if the Lord is truly speaking to you.

Fourth, God's Word is totally sufficient for all of our needs. We don't need anything else. In 2 Timothy 3:16-17 it reads "All Scripture is given by inspiration of God, and is profitable for doctrine, for reproof, for correction, for instruction in righteousness, that the man of God may be complete, thoroughly equipped for every good work." We Christians can be totally secure in the Lord by studying the Bible because it is God's plan for our life.

And fifth, the Word of God will accomplish what it promises. If God told you something will happen, and you wait, it will happen. In Isaiah 55:11 it says, "So shall My word be that goes forth from My mouth; It shall not return to Me void, but it shall accomplish what I please, and it shall prosper in the thing for which I sent it." God sent His word to accomplish His perfect will in our lives. If God makes a promise to you He will fulfill it in His own time. There are so many promises given to us in the Bible. These promises reassure us and bring comfort to our lives in our times of trial. I challenge you to take time to study the Word of God. The Lord will show you wonderful things that will change your life.

## FELLOWSHIP AND ASSOCIATIONS

It is easier to succeed in anything especially when you're in the same company of people doing the same thing like you. If you stay in the company of businessmen, it is liable that you will automatically become a businessman. If you join the company of prophets, you'll soon become a prophet. Therefore, for you to be connected, you have to make a conscious act to stay connected to fellowships and associations that will help keep you on track. For, iron sharpeneth iron.

*For where two or three gathers in my name, there am I with them."*
*(Matthew 18:20)*

*not giving up meeting together, as some are in the habit of doing, but encouraging one another—and all the more as you see the Day approaching. (Hebrews 10:25)*

## WALK WITH GOD.

What does it mean to walk with God? In Genesis 5:22-24,

*After he became the father of Methuselah, Enoch walked faithfully with God 300 years and had other sons and daughters. Altogether, Enoch lived a total of 365 years. Enoch walked faithfully with God; then he was no more because God took him away. (Genesis 5:22-24)*

Walk with God is walking in the spirit. It is a continuous step. It is a kind of continuous stage of spiritual consciousness. A state whereby you're aware of God. You in constant communication with Him. It is in this stage whereby you are able to overcome the lust of the flesh. You will be fully drawn in God and enjoy the supernatural flow of the spirit and presence of God.

The Bible said that Enoch walks with God, that means you got to a point in your relationship with God that He tells you what to do and what not to do. For an example, you set out to go and buy a car and God is saying to you, not that one, not that one either but this one here. Maybe you are about to get offended and God comforts you by saying, don't be offended, change your emotion and start laughing. Sometimes, I find myself in such situations when my children are crying I encourage them to cry a little bit more and then later I instruct them to start laughing and that's all the whole event will tend into fun. God as a father is able to change you at a moment, intercept your emotion, your concept, your will, and make you smile. If you vehemently follow only your own will and decision, you might be driving to the pit of hell, that is He must be able to tell you to stop, turn back and take another route and instruct you to go back home. Let further take a critical look about Enoch.

## ENOCH WALKED WITH GOD

The analogy of walking and the Christian life is used throughout Scripture. But what does it mean to walk with God? It is not merely living by rules and regulations or making daily resolutions that we quickly break. It is much more than that. The prophet Amos revealed an important truth about what it means to walk with God when he asked, "Can two walk together, unless they are agreed?" (Amos 3:3 NKJV). The word he used for "together" gives the idea of two people moving in rhythm together, as in riding a tandem bicycle. But it is not about getting God into rhythm with us; it is getting ourselves into rhythm with Him. That is what it means to walk with God.

## ENOCH WAS WELL-PLEASING TO GOD

Hebrews 11:5 says, "He had this testimony, that he pleased God" (NKJV). Sometimes we have the mistaken notion that God is very hard to please. Yet God knows our weaknesses and frailties better than anyone, and He is not as hard to please as we might think.

So how do we please God? God is pleased when, in spite of the fact that we are in the right, we patiently endure when misunderstood (1 Peter 2:19-20). When you do what is right and patiently endure suffering for it, that is called meekness, and it pleases God. God is also pleased when children obey their parents (Colossians 3:20); when we worship Him, and help others (Hebrews 13:15-16); and when we give financially to the work of the kingdom (Philippians 4:17-18).

## ENOCH WAS A WITNESS FOR GOD

Enoch walked with God, he was well-pleasing to God, and lastly, he was a witness for God. As Enoch walked with God and pleased Him, he had a testimony and a witness. Every Christian has a testimony. People are watching us. They are observing us. And we should give a lot of thought to that. Before we can effectively witness for God, we must first walk with Him.

## PRAY IN THE SPIRIT

Praying in the spirit, Romans 8:26

*In the same way, the Spirit helps us in our weakness. We do not know what we ought to pray for, but the Spirit himself intercedes for us through wordless groans. (Romans 8:26)*

Sincerely we don't know what to pray as we ought to pray, it is the spirit that will guide and teach us the what to pray as we ought. Note, the above verse didn't say we don't know how to pray, but rather we don't know what to pray. How to pray and what to pray are two different things. We have briefly described how to pray or the manner to pray. Jesus taught us the how to pray, He said we have to pray to the Father who is in Heaven, not praying to Jesus but to the Father in the name of Jesus through the Holy Spirit. The father hears your prayer when you pray in the name of Jesus and via the power of the Holy Spirit. This is the how to pray.

As you get to the concluding part of this book, let me briefly describe to you the what to pray. The bible says we don't know what to pray as we ought but it is the spirit that helps and enables us in this. Why? The spirit knows all things and searches the heart and mind of men. He knows the will of the father for us. He helps pray his will our life through praying in the spirit and many others way. Also, the spirit knows the end from the beginning, He knows the future, he can see in the future. He can see the accident that has been planned by your enemy for you to die. So, in prayers, he reveals that for you to pray against it. Note He's not going to stop but he would lead you to pray against because all authority has been handed to you by Christ Jesus. That is why praying in the spirit and with the spirit is awesome and powerful.

As you conclude and drop this book remember, you need the Holy as your ultimate guide and personal mentor for a transformed life. If you haven't received him, I ask you to just kneel wherever you are and ask God the Father to send you the Holy Spirit. You won't ask the Father for the Spirit and He gives you a snake. No! He will give you His Spirit which will dwell in you and make you a conqueror. Life without the Spirit of God is Horror. Stay connected! Stay transformed! Stay blessed! You're a chosen generation and not a generation of vipers. Go and transform others!

God bless you.

www.ingramcontent.com/pod-product-compliance
Lightning Source LLC
Chambersburg PA
CBHW032104080426
42733CB00006B/415